Our Kind of People

Our Kind of People

The Story of the First 50 Years at
Benton & Bowles

By
Gordon Webber

Inquiries should be addressed to: Benton & Bowles, Inc., 909 Third Avenue, New York, New York 10022

Printed in the United States of America

Library of Congress Number: 79-55490
ISBN: 0-9603040-1-0

Designed by George H. Buehler/Blair McFadden

*For all members of the
Benton & Bowles family—
past, present and future*

BOOKS BY GORDON WEBBER

Years of Eden

The Far Shore

What End but Love

The Great Buffalo Hotel

Our Kind of People:
The Story of the First
50 Years at
Benton & Bowles

CONTENTS

Acknowledgments

This history was made possible, in very large degree, by the people who have given so generously of their time, advice and professional help.

I want especially to thank Vic Bloede for his counsel and for his skillful editing, as well as for the insights into the B&B story that only his perspective could provide. His help and encouragement in every phase of the project were indispensable.

Special thanks also are due to Jack Bowen and Al Hampel for their support and guidance; and to Ted Steele whose 37-year view of the agency's history was uniquely illuminating. I am grateful, too, for valuable help from Frank Smith who, in 1968—69, assembled a large amount of historical material about the agency on which I drew extensively.

The help of A.M. Gilbert is also much appreciated. He provided essential facts and dates (he was almost the only one who could conjure up dates), as well as a fund of stories and observations reflecting his 35-year association as legal counsel to the agency. To Phil Reiss, special thanks for reading the manuscript and hazarding the opinion that nothing in it is libelous.

The almost daily assistance over a period of several months of Chief Librarian Lois Burke and the staff of the B&B library—Muriel Barnes, Mei Lee and Mary Drummond—was efficient and cheerfully given, and I am forever in their debt.

An important part of the history is the pictorial sections, and I want to thank Dick Ende for his help in selecting this material, and for his design and layout. Thanks also to David Kreinik for integrating and overseeing all the details involved in the printing of the book.

I want to thank Sylvia Usher, Myrtle Selders and Peggy McSorley for their friendly and efficient secretarial help; and also Linda Seibert and my two former secretaries, Rosemarie Leone (now a copywriter) and Barbara Cole; as well as Netta Valdimer; Helen Keyes and her messenger staff; Frank Topham, Pat Duley, Vera Sands, Pam Richards, Diane Cervellone and Barbara Bellow Watson.

Also, the people in public relations were most helpful: Charlotte Kelly and Susan Whelan at the start of the project, and later, Joan Aho, Sue Glick and Susan Farrell.

A large part of the book consists of the stories, recollections and experiences of present and former members of the B&B family, and others. I want to thank them all for the help they gave me with interviews, conversations, correspondence, scripts, screenings, research material, commercials, ads and photographs. Their names are listed in the notes on sources.

One

The Beginning Years
1929–31

*"I don't think we'd have started if we'd known what
was going to happen."*

Chester Bowles, in an
interview October 1978

*T*he *New York Times* of July 15, 1929 carried a
front page story about the bankruptcy of the private banking firm of
Clarke Brothers in which eventual payment to creditors "might be as
little as 5 cents on the dollar." Yet on the same day the stock market
rose to an all-time high. Only the gloomiest of forecasters had any
foreboding of the crash that was to come three months later, which
Variety would headline: WALL STREET LAYS AN EGG.

Certainly no foreboding was felt by the two young Yale men,
William Benton and Chester Bowles, who on that pleasant mid-
summer day—it was St. Swithin's day, the temperature in the 80's—
opened an advertising agency in a two-room office on the 29th floor
of the Chanin building at Lexington Avenue and 42nd Street. They
had scraped together $12,000 between them, and their staff included,
in addition to themselves, a secretary, an office boy and a young man
just out of college. They had persuaded Ralph Starr Butler, advertising director of General Foods, to entrust them with two small accounts, Hellmann's Mayonnaise and Certo, a pectin extract for making jellies, with a combined advertising budget for the rest of the year
of $60,000. It was the beginning of a relationship between General
Foods and Benton & Bowles that continues to this day, with the
$60,000 billing growing, by 1979, to $62 million worldwide.

"Actually, the Depression helped us," said Bowles recently,
recalling the beginning days of the young agency. "Clients were worried about their business and looking for new ideas they weren't getting from the old-line agencies."

Benton made the same point on a radio interview in 1970:

> Desperate advertisers, desperately worried, said, "By
> George, maybe we'd better listen to these young men
> who've got these new ideas" . . . I don't think we could
> have built that business during the boom years of the
> 1920s.

William Burnett Benton began his advertising career in 1922
at one of the old-line agencies, the New York branch of Chicago-
based Lord & Thomas. His salary was $25 a week. In a jubilant letter
to his mother he said he had a job "with the most successful agency
in the country with such accounts as Quaker Oats, Pepsodent and
Palmolive Soap."*'

His mother, Emma Benton, head of Hosmer Hall, a private
girls' school in St. Louis, was not pleased. "Dear Billy," she wrote,
"I'm sorry to hear you are going into a business that says 'Palmolive
Soap is a good soap.' "

Even with budgeting a dollar a day for meals, and having only
a candy bar for breakfast, Benton found he couldn't make ends meet.
To improve his financial situation, he moved: first, to Charles W.
Hoyt, then to a $50-a-week copywriting job at George Batten Com-
pany—later Batten, Barton, Durstine & Osborne (a name Jack Benny
once said "sounded like a trunk falling down stairs").

His progress at Batten was rapid. He soon got a $1,000-a-year
raise and management said it hoped "he'd be with us for a long time."
But despite his success, as he wrote Emma, he was "often filled with
indescribable longings." As far back as 1924 he was yearning for a
different kind of life than the one advertising offered. "As I read of
the Teapot Dome scandal in Washington," he wrote Emma, "I have
the overwhelming desire to get into politics.**

Meanwhile, he continued to get ahead at Batten. Impressed by
his energies and abilities, the management made him head of the trade

---

*Devoted son that he was, Benton wrote his mother at least once a week, often daily, for many
years. The more than two million words of these letters, many of which contain details of his
business career, are an important source for the early years of this history.

**This ambition would have to wait some twenty years for fulfillment, until 1945, when he
became a member of a delegation studying preliminary approaches to the United Nations conference. He later became Assistant Secretary of State in the Truman Administration, and, briefly,
U.S. Senator from Connecticut.

advertising department, and later put him in charge of hiring and training all copywriters for the company. With his increased work load he found he needed an assistant and finally found one through Yale's placement bureau. He described the new recruit in a letter to Emma: "He has very little experience, just having graduated from Yale last year. He is right for this business, as he was captain of the golf team at Yale, and is from one of the oldest New England families. . . . He's either going to be a tremendous success in advertising or a tragic flop."

The $25-a-week assistant was Chester Bowles.

After attempts to get a job in journalism, then in the Department of Commerce, Bowles, who was two years behind Benton at Yale, had decided to go into business, promising himself that "I would leave when I was 35."

"Chet" Bowles and "Bill" Benton soon became close friends. In March Benton wrote Emma: "Chet is most likable and is already popular with all the boys in my department. Tonight at dinner he was talking about the possibility of our going into business together in four or five years."

Benton had been with Batten for three years, when on a Saturday morning in May (the standard work week then was 5½ or 6 days) he was called in and fired. The reason: "disloyalty" to the Batten firm for campaigning with a barrage of memos (a habit he was to be addicted to all his life) urging a merger between Batten and a young agency in the same building: Barton, Durstine & Osborne. He was given a week to pack up and leave.*

With Benton's departure, the Batten Company faced internal revolt. Benton regularly wore a white carnation in his lapel; after he was fired, members of his department took up the same custom (someone must have known his English history, his War of Roses), in loyalty to their departed chief. Sterling Getchell, a star copywriter, had cards printed with "Aw Nuts" on them, left one on each executive's desk and walked out, eventually to start his own agency.

---

*Charlie Brower, later to become president and chairman of the board of BBDO, had been hired by Benton just before he was fired. When Brower arrived to find Benton gone, he told someone that he'd resigned his job to take this one and was ready to go to work. He was asked: "How much did Benton agree to pay you?" Brower subsequently confessed that in answering the question "I gave myself my first raise."

Within two months the Batten management acted on Benton's suggestion. Sometime later, Benton said, "I should have been given a million-dollar check as a 'finder's fee' for coming up with the idea of a merger of Batten and BD&O."

Benton had several job offers, but felt his old firm of Lord & Thomas—then the largest in the country—was the best place to learn the management skills he needed to make the eventual move to his own agency. He went to work at Lord & Thomas's Chicago office as assistant general manager, and in six months was earning $25,000, double his salary at Batten.

But his sights were still set on going into business for himself. From the beginning, his first choice of a partner was Bowles, who had the original idea. But along the way at least two other partners were considered. Sterling Getchell, by this time at J. Walter Thompson, was eager to strike out on his own. Charles Mortimer, then in the advertising department of General Foods (which he would eventually head) considered the possibility, but finally rejected it. Mortimer, however, did offer to put in a good word for Benton and his prospective partner, Bowles, with Ralph Starr Butler.

"A 10–to–1 Chance"

The first presentation of the new advertising team-to-be was made early in 1929 by Bowles, while Benton was still in Chicago. It was Bowles's conviction, he told Butler of General Foods, that many agencies placed too much emphasis on the statistics of market research and not enough on the creative job. He described the improved service and source of fresh ideas he could expect from a young, hungry agency struggling to make its mark. Butler was favorably impressed, although concerned that Bowles was so young—he was 28. After subsequent meetings between Butler, Mortimer, Bowles and Benton, Butler said the chances were "10–to–1" they could expect at least one account.

Confident that he and Bowles "could make a go of things," regardless of whether they got the GF account, Benton submitted his resignation. When Albert Lasker, mercurial owner of Lord & Thomas, heard Benton planned to leave, he offered to double his salary to $50,000 if he would stay.

"Why, Mr. Lasker," Benton said, smiling. "Do you mean to tell me I'm worth fifty thousand a year while you've been paying me only twenty-five? Why, you've been taking *my* money!" Lasker laughed, said he was sorry to see him go, but wished him luck. He had taken over ownership of Lord & Thomas at an early age himself, and could understand a man wanting to have his own business.

Instead of one account, Butler awarded the young team two. He had the same "young man" theory of business as John Orr Young, cofounder of Young & Rubicam, who wrote in *Adventures in Advertising:* "If you are lucky enough to find some young man with the special energy and daring which leads him into business for himself, you will benefit from having that incalculably valuable quality serving you."

The fledgling advertising team had decided Benton would handle the account work—as early as his first job with Lord & Thomas, Benton wrote his mother, "I don't think I'll set the world on fire writing copy." Bowles was to do the creative work. (At Batten he had worked on Wonder Bread with Charlie Brower, who later wrote that Bowles's headlines always began "Madam, please. . . ," "Madam, we guarantee. . . ." "It didn't bother Chet a bit," Brower said, "that there are various kinds of madams.")

After being critical of research, the first major project of the new agency was a consumer survey for Certo. Both Bill and Chet believed that surveys were frequently misused, too often having no influence on advertising. They would change all that. Benton, almost accidentally, had invented consumer research in 1928 while working for Lasker at Lord & Thomas. (Before that there was only market research.) Lasker, who had nothing but contempt for research—he said "it was simply something that told you a jackass has two ears" —nevertheless had needed a survey to impress a client. He asked Benton to take on the job.

"What do you want me to survey?" Benton asked.

"I don't give a damn what you survey," Lasker said. "All I want is the biggest one ever made."

The massive door-to-door survey Benton came up with—it ran to four volumes—impressed everyone, even Lasker, and was the first major study of *consumer* attitudes in contrast to *market* data.

Using the same canvassing technique, the new agency made a nationwide investigation of jam- and jelly-making habits—Bill and Chet and their wives even went out and rang doorbells—and the results formed the basis of the first Certo campaign: half-page, four-color magazine ads featuring winners of jelly-making contests at state fairs. With art supervision by Jim Balch, the agency's lone art director, the Certo advertising drew much favorable attention and substantially increased Certo sales.

The Drunkest Desk in the East

Balch, a moody, gifted man, was the source of many stories. A man who liked to have a drink when he wanted it, he found Prohibition inconvenient, to say the least, but also found a way around it, as many Americans did. He designed and had built a special outsize desk for his office which had a secret compartment large enough to accommodate a case of whiskey. (The desk, inherited by Bill Tompkins, present head of the art studio, survived until the agency's move to Third Avenue.)

Balch was also devoted to practical jokes, as so many advertising practitioners seemed to have been before the business got so serious and disciplined. One Christmas he had constructed for a freelance artist friend a jigsaw puzzle, the picture of which was a pornographic scene of a man and woman *in flagrante delicto*, with the man's head airbrushed out and the artist's head substituted. Comes Christmas morning, and the artist's wife and kiddies gather around the tree to open presents. The thoughtful gift from Balch is unwrapped and the family begins to assemble the puzzle. As the picture emerges—consternation! The kiddies are shooed from the room. Wild accusations from the wife! It was well into the new year before she would speak to him again. (History fails to record what the artist said—or did—to Balch.)

One more bit of Balchiana: He once was asked, under protest, to share his office, already bulging with the booze-concealing desk, with a newly hired art director. In the days that followed a smell began to pervade the office, a smell so foul it made the senses reel. Every day, as Balch worked unconcernedly at his desk, the baffled AD searched for the source of the overpowering stench, muttering that it smelled like *fish*. And indeed it was, as he finally discovered. Balch had thumbtacked a fish to the underside of his unwanted roommate's chair.

The Certo state fair campaign gave rise to the agency's first public relations operation. Norman Klein, a former reporter on the *New York Evening World*, was the first drumbeater. He left journalism, he said, because at 33 and with a family to support, he "wanted to make a few bucks"—his salary was $8,000, more than double the salary of a newspaper man in the '30s. (A reporter, so to speak, who came in from the cold.) Trading murders and fires for prize-winning jelly, Klein covered the state fair circuit, placing stories, with discreet Certo mentions, in local papers around the country.

Toward the end of its first year the agency, after soliciting some ten accounts, succeeded in landing two: National Union, a maker of radio tubes and a competitor of RCA, and Squibb for two small products, Lentheric perfumes and a new antiseptic.

Benton, turning to his mother in St. Louis for help in selecting a name for the Squibb antiseptic, sent her a list of sixteen names and asked her to "tell the girls . . . to study them one minute" before writing down the name they liked best. "All material must be in my hands by next Monday," Benton wrote with his characteristic brusque efficiency. Whether Emma interrupted her classes to conduct the test is not known. But none of the names Benton sent her included the one eventually selected, Di-phen.

The year ended with seventeen people on staff, just $40,000 in billings (the original appropriations had been cut), and everybody working day and night to keep the little firm afloat. "I was up until after three o'clock last night," Benton wrote Emma, "and have been for eight or ten days, trying to put through the 1930 plans for General Foods."

The Depression Deepens

By 1930 the Depression had begun to penetrate the fabric of the nation's economy like a wintry wind blowing through the ragged coat of a Bowery derelict. The banks—those that were still in business —had taken over many companies, and one of the most promising sources of new business assignments the agency had developed was Lehman Brothers.

An especially attractive Lehman Brothers plum was Helena Rubinstein, which Madame Rubinstein had sold two years before at the peak of the boom. Now the stock was down to a few cents a share, and Lehman Brothers had named Guy Lemmon, an experienced marketing man, as general manager. The banking firm assigned to the agency both Helena Rubinstein and Adolph Goebel Meats—another Depression-beleaguered firm—but the associations were short-lived. After the agency had completed a $65,000 "Certo-type" research study of women's attitudes toward cosmetics, and prepared advertising, Madame Rubinstein reappeared on the scene and decided she wanted her company back. She bought controlling interest, kicked out the bankers and Guy Lemmon and, for good measure, fired Benton & Bowles as well. It looked for a while as though the agency was out its $65,000, but eventually Madame paid.

Adolph Goebel lasted only long enough for one memorable ad to see the light of day:

FOR EVERY POUND OF GOEBEL'S

MEAT YOU BUY, WE'LL GIVE 1¢

TOWARD REPEAL OF PROHIBITION

It didn't help. The Depression finally so depressed Goebel's sales that it dropped its advertising.

Despite these disturbing losses, 1930 saw a modest improvement of the agency's position. In April it moved to larger quarters at 5 East 45th Street where the furniture was designed by Jim Balch (presumably *sans* concealed liquor compartments) and custom-built, as Benton wrote Emma, "for 50 percent of what we could purchase the cheapest furniture on 6th Avenue." And generally, there was a note of optimism about the business in Benton's faithful letters to his mother. In October he wrote: "Bad business conditions . . . are good ones as far as we are concerned. It is in bad times that advertisers think most about changing their agencies. I do not see how we can possibly net less than $100,000 next year (1931), and it's very probable that we may net as much as $200,000."

Early in 1931 Chet Bowles got a call from International Silver. Would he be interested in the William Rogers silverware account? Bowles knew Young & Rubicam was handling the business and decided to talk to them before giving an answer. He called Raymond Rubicam and told him about the call from their disaffected client. This was the beginning of a close and amicable relationship between the two agencies that has continued for half a century. While there has always been hearty competition between them, and they've not been above an occasional raid on each other's staffs, the two agencies have enjoyed a kind of "spiritual kinship" (they are about the same age; Y&R was founded in 1925), and a long history of cooperation on projects of their mutual clients, General Foods and Procter & Gamble.

Later the agency agreed to take the International Silver account which, although small, helped assuage the pain of the Rubinstein disappointment.

A Dangerous Proposal

Vic Bloede has said, "We tell the client the truth, even if it hurts."

This reputation for candor had its genesis in the early days of the agency's relationship with General Foods on the Hellmann's account. Riding the Hellmann's delivery trucks in Brooklyn, Benton had concluded that the delivery system was inefficient and costly. Moreover, sales volume in many sections of Hellmann's franchise was too low to return a profit. So the agency made a radical recommendation: that GF sell Hellmann's Mayonnaise to the Gold Dust subsidiary, Best Foods, which was more knowledgeable about marketing the perishable product and already had an extensive and profitable franchise west of the Rockies.

After making the recommendation, "Chet and Bill were a little scared," according to an early account. They felt a merger was right for GF, but that it probably meant they would lose the business. They were more than a little scared when GF acted on their recommendation and sold Hellmann's to Best Foods.

"What happens now?" a worried Benton asked Colby Chester. "Are we out?" Chester, impressed with Benton's objective reporting of the Hellmann's problem, told him he'd see what could be done. He called Randolph Catlin, president of Gold Dust, and urged him to retain B&B as the agency for Hellmann's after the sale to Best Foods. Catlin did even better than that: He gave B&B all the Best Foods business, which included Best Foods Mayonnaise and Nucoa margarine. There were some initial reservations about the mandated marriage by the Best Foods people, but they were dispelled when they saw the agency's first creative work, and Best Foods president Jay Gould became an enthusiastic supporter of B&B.

Telling the truth, even if it hurts, doesn't always pay off so handsomely—in this case, it increased agency billing about $700,000 —but, as future events will show, it is probably always better than expediency.

"It's His Glands"

Bill Benton was destined from the beginning to succeed in everything he did. A Puritan pioneer background, and a strong-willed mother who expected him always to do his best, shaped him into an early achiever who never stopped. He was intensely ambitious and energetic, with a remarkable physical constitution—he could get by on three hours' sleep a night.

"It's his glands," said his Swedish-born friend Anton Carlson, the psychologist, during W.W. II. "If ve could find oudt vat makes Benton go, and inject a liddle in efferybody, ve could vin de vawr in a veek!"

Early B&Bers remember him as a man always on the go. "He was strictly business," said Eddie Schneeberg, who began with the agency in August 1929 as Bowles's first office boy.

"He could do, and often did, four things at once," Schneeberg recalls. "Hold a meeting, dictate a memo, get his nails manicured and order liquor from his bootlegger, a little man who used to come to the office on East 45th Street with samples in a black suitcase."

Julie King, a former publicity writer, remembered her first day at the agency in April 1932 when she was stationed at a long table outside Benton's office. There she could observe the frantic coming and going of people in and out of his office, the loud arguments, the bursts of temper. She said she was "firmly convinced after three hours that Mr. Benton had high blood pressure and that Mr. Hobler, who *did* look like a doctor, was his personal physician."

"The dictating machine—the Iron Lady, we called it—that's what I remember most about Benton," says Helen Scofield, secretary to two presidents, who retired in 1974 after forty years with the agency. "He had a dictating machine at home, too," she recalls. "He'd arrive in the morning and Mary Kelly, who did his transcribing, would say, 'Oh, my God, how many has he got today?' And there'd be a dozen or so cylinders he'd dictated the night before." Everybody in the agency got Benton memos: a steady stream of suggestions, comments, criticisms and complaints which his associates came to dread. (An early associate recalls that Benton's cannonade of correspondence "ran Hobler ragged.")

Bertha Tallman, in charge of the steno pool (stenographers were not permitted to sit in the offices of the men; Benton thought it "invited trouble"), used to hold off routing the more caustic memos —they got sharper and more critical as the evening wore on toward midnight—until she was sure, in the cold light of day, he really wanted to send them.

One time someone in the mailroom accidentally shaved several of Benton's cylinders before they were transcribed. "He was fit to be tied," recalls Ed Mead, then a $15-a-week mailroom boy. "Wanted to fire us all."

After Benton left the agency and was at the University of Chicago, his associates were amazed to see him, in the middle of a conference on inter-American relations, break off, grab his dictating machine and say, "Get somebody to give me a memorandum on what this philosophy of Thomas Aquinas is all about," then jump back into inter-American relations.

Benton was an early enthusiast of air travel and, it was said, took the train between New York and Chicago only when he needed a haircut; he couldn't spare the time for one anywhere else. He is probably the only man who delayed the departure of the Twentieth-Century Limited. According to legend, an office boy threw himself across the tracks in front of the train at Grand Central station until Bill and Chet, on their way to make a new business presentation, arrived with their charts.*

A brilliant, original man, he was obsessively goal-oriented, and from the beginning those goals lay ultimately beyond advertising.

In March 1930 Benton wrote Emma, "My problem within a few years will very probably be to find men to bring into the firm who can buy me out and carry on the business." He even discussed the idea with a client. "Clare," he once said to Clarence Francis of General Foods, "how do I get out of this industry?" He looked forward to the time, he wrote Emma, when he could "retire with an income of $15,000 to $20,000 and devote myself to some other form of activity."**

"Chet Had the Warmth"

While Benton thought of goals, Bowles thought of people. He always had his feelers out. Comparing the former partners, advertising man Chet LaRoche said, "Bowles can play by ear. Benton can't." Clarence Francis, retired chairman of the board of General Foods, still standing tall and erect in his 91st year, said recently, "I knew them both well, Chet and Bill. Bill had a keen mind, he was an amazing

---

*The Benton new-business charts were famous in their time. One, showing how the agency had prospered despite the Depression, was in the form of an X: one line, representing the stock market performance, ran from upper left corner to lower right; B&B's billings ran from lower left to upper right.

**His goal was modest. His fortune from his ownership of Encyclopaedia Britannica and Muzak, among other enterprises, eventually totaled, according to Fortune magazine, between $150 and $200 million dollars.

fellow. But Chet had the warmth. He was always thinking about the welfare of his people."

Bowles, in the early days of the agency, was a vigorous, athletic man, a scratch golf player and a good sailor—for many years he skippered his own 72-foot schooner.* "A tall, affable, loosely-coupled Connecticut Yankee," one magazine writer called him, "with a big chin and a famous starboard smile." In client meetings, according to Francis, "he was quiet, thoughtful, asked a lot of questions. He was very objective, always wanted your opinion." "There was none of the huckster about him," another early associate recalled. "He knew what he was talking about and he said it simply and directly. What he said, you believed."

Bowles's concern for people he worked with was genuine and went beyond a decent boss's desire to try to keep his troops happy. He spent a good deal of time helping young copywriters improve their skills. He sought out and hired the best people he could find. The reputation the agency had built by the mid-'30s of being "a hot young agency" was largely Chet's creation.

"He was a kind person, with decent instincts," said another associate. "When a workman who was doing some work in Chet's office left his tools there overnight and they were stolen, Chet gave the man $200 to buy a new set."

He had a special relationship with his office boy, Eddie Schneeberg. The bright, brash son of a Brooklyn grocer, with more than a little of his mother's Irish wit, Schneeberg began working for Bowles fresh out of high school for $10 a week. In the beginning years, during the Depression and the New Deal, he was the office radical, and used to have spirited debates with Bowles on issues of the day.

"He got me to read the *Daily Worker*," Bowles said. "I used to send Bonnie Cox, my secretary, over to Third Avenue to buy it. She'd come back with it hidden inside *The New York Times*."

---

*Al Stanford, a former B&Ber, recalled recently a memorable sail with Bowles on his schooner, the *Nordleys*, in 1941. "We were coming back from Bermuda and got caught in a hurricane that kept looping back on us. We battled the blow for seventeen days. Half our sails were carried away and we were reported lost in the papers. But Chet brought her through and sailed into the Connecticut River, right up to the front lawn of his house at Hayden's Point."

Schneeberg once gave a speech in the lobby of B&B's building at 444 Madison in support of striking elevator operators.

"Hobe wanted to fire me," Schneeberg said, "but Chet wouldn't let him."

Schneeberg was fired some time after that—"while I was out of town," Bowles said—but he was subsequently rehired by Bowles and eventually became a top copywriter and head of the radio copy department.

"The only time I saw Chet get mad," Schneeberg said, "was over the golf shoes."

Golf shoes?

"He got a new pair and asked me to have the spikes put on, and I took them over to a shoe man on Third Avenue. Neither of us, of course, knew anything about golf, and he put all the spikes on the soles and none on the heels. Boy, did Chet cuss me out!"

The election of 1932 produced strong anti-Democrat feelings among the agency's predominantly Republican clients. One major client, fearful of what would happen to the country if Roosevelt were elected, urged Benton to call his staff together and *tell* them, by God, to vote for Hoover. A meeting was scheduled and Benton was dutifully set to do what the client wanted when Bowles got wind of it. He persuaded his partner that it was a bad idea and the meeting was called off.

Altogether, 1931 was a disappointing year from the standpoint of billings. The economic plight of the country had its crippling effects even on packaged food products, which were thought to be largely depression-proof. (Advertising appropriations in the U.S. had dropped from $3.4 billion in 1929 to $1.6 billion by the mid-'30s.)

"Business isn't as bright as I wish it was," Benton wrote his mother. "The depression has cut billing on Squibb to the vanishing point . . . even General Foods expenditures have been reduced."

Instead of netting $100,000 or $200,000, as Benton had hoped, net earnings for 1931 ended up at $28,000 on a gross income of $166,000, 20 percent off the previous year.

But brighter days were ahead. The new year would see a dramatic development in the fortunes of B&B that in one stroke would place it among the top agencies in the country.

Two
Enter Hobe
1932–35

General Foods president Colby Chester was unhappy.

Erwin, Wasey, the agency that handled six GF products billing about $5 million dollars, had just landed the $10-million dollar Camel account, and Chester felt his products weren't getting the attention they deserved.

Erwin, Wasey had won the cigarette assignment on the basis of its speculative campaign for launching a dramatic innovation: the first cigarette package to be wrapped in the new DuPont invention, cellophane. For weeks top Erwin, Wasey people had been closeted in the Drake Hotel in Chicago preparing advertising, media and strategy plans. The glamor account was monopolizing the time and attention of just about everybody at the agency and Colby Chester, like any neglected client, didn't like it one bit.

One of the top people involved in the Camel push was the account supervisor on Erwin, Wasey's GF business, a man destined to become a focal figure—some would even say father figure—in the life of Benton & Bowles: Atherton Wells Hobler.

Hobler—or Hobe as he was known to most people—was 41 at the time: tall, restlessly energetic, dark-haired, with hypnotic, slightly protuberant brown eyes behind rimless glasses, eyes one associate said were like "X-ray eyes—they seemed to bore right through you." Of German ancestry—his great-grandfather left Bavaria for America in 1801 to escape Napoleon—he was born and reared in the farming center of Batavia, Illinois, where he followed his father as sales and advertising manager of the Appleton Implement Company, after a brief time at the Gardner Advertising Company in St. Louis.

From an early age Hobler showed the traits of resourcefulness, enterprise and strong single-minded purpose that were to mark the steady upward course of his career. As his former partner Chester Bowles recently remarked with a wry smile, "Hobe had a brilliant one-track mind." In 1917, through a bonus arrangement he devised for himself at Appleton, he earned $9,000, more than the general manager of the company. The owner was appalled. As Hobler later recalled, "He told me I was making entirely too much money for a man only twenty-six years old."

When the owner wanted to reduce his salary to a flat $6,000 with no bonus, Hobler quit and returned to Gardner in St. Louis where he worked on Ralston Purina and met the original, innovative founder of the company, William Danford. (It was Danford, a W.W. I hero, who adopted the doughboys' word "chow" for Purina products, created the famous checkerboard trademark, and first introduced the idea of brand managers.)

In 1919 Hobler met for the first time a man who was to play an important role in B&B's history—Clarence Francis, then sales manager of Ralston's cereal division. It was Francis, after he became vice-president of the Postum Company in 1921, who urged Hobler to move to New York, which he eventually did, joining Erwin, Wasey in 1925 to handle the Postum account. Francis, recently recalling that meeting, said, "I first thought he was just another smooth advertising type—he had those very earnest eyes—but we soon became fast friends."

The fortunes of Erwin, Wasey-New York prospered even as the Depression worsened—its $25-million billings in 1931 were the largest of any single agency office in the country—and Hobler shared in the prosperity. By then he owned 22 percent of the company stock and his income in 1931 was in the six-figure range.

But despite this largesse, Hobler was not happy.

He was not happy about his relationship with Arthur Kudner, a principal along with Wasey and Obie Winters. "Art Kudner and I were two very strong-minded individuals," Hobler wrote later, "and I questioned whether one agency could long hold us both."

And he was not happy for the same reason Colby Chester was

not happy: he wasn't getting the creative work he wanted on the General Foods products he supervised.

A Fateful Luncheon

Then one of those seemingly minor incidents occurred that set in motion a crucial chain of events. Hobler described it in his unpublished autobiography:

> Obie Winters and Art Kudner invited . . . Ralph Butler to luncheon at the Cloud Club in the Chrysler Building. Ralph was pleased to accept because he had a copy problem he wanted to discuss with Obie and Art. On the way to the dining room, Winters bought a newspaper with the noon quotations of the New York Stock Exchange. Little was accomplished at luncheon. Winters spent most of the time with his head buried in the newspaper . . . it was quite obvious that both men were more interested in the prices of the stocks they owned than in Ralph Butler's copy problem.

Hobler, hearing of this fateful luncheon from his friend Clare Francis, saw a way out of both his problems, and went into action. He arranged a meeting with Francis and Butler at which he told them he was resigning from Erwin, Wasey. He asked Butler if he "would continue to desire my services on the company accounts I was supervising."

Butler, a gentle, soft-spoken, scholarly man (he taught the country's first marketing course at the University of Wisconsin), assured him that he would.

"I asked Ralph Butler what he would think about my talking to Bill Benton and Chet Bowles." Butler thought it was an excellent idea.

But before Hobler talked to Benton and Bowles, Butler called Benton and asked him to drop in and see him and Clare Francis. He asked Benton if he felt B&B was in a position to take on the GF business being handled by Erwin, Wasey. Knowing the new assignment would nearly triple the agency's billings, but also knowing it wasn't staffed to handle it, Benton reluctantly said he didn't think so. Then Butler suggested an alternative plan, and discussed the possibility of a partnership with Hobler, pointing out that Hobler's maturity and experience could be a big asset to B&B. Butler also said that if Benton and Bowles shied away from a partnership with Hobler, GF would still give the agency half the accounts at Erwin, Wasey. The other half would go with Hobler who would seek a partnership with another agency.

"I propose . . . a new advertising agency. . . ."

Hobler, holding what can only be called a winning hand with a couple of aces up his sleeves, had dinner with Benton. The two former midwesterners (Benton was originally from Minnesota) got along well, and they set a second meeting at which Hobler made a proposal:

> I proposed that we incorporate a new advertising agency in which Benton, Bowles and I hold an identical share of stock: one-third interest in the agency for each principal. Bill reacted with surprise to this proposal . . . because it offered him the same share . . . that I wanted (and) because it provided the same interest . . . in the agency to Chet Bowles, the creative head of the would-be organization. . . .

Benton had assumed that Hobler, with $5 million in billings in his pocket, would want more than a third share.

Bowles was on vacation in Bermuda during these preliminary negotiations, but was kept informed by cable. When he returned and heard the specific terms of the new partnership, he at first, in Hobler's words, was "truculent about my proposals." He questioned the idea of equal partnerships, and also the right Hobler had to add his name to the firm name if he chose to. As it later developed, Bowles thought Benton, not Hobler, was responsible for bringing in the Erwin, Wasey share of the General Foods business. With this misunderstanding cleared up, the new partnership was consummated. In April 1932 the firm was incorporated and a "new" Benton & Bowles was born.

Within a few months all the GF accounts Hobler had handled at Erwin, Wasey—Maxwell House Coffee, Post Toasties, Post Bran

Flakes, Diamond Crystal Salt, Walter Baker's Cocoa and Chocolate and Log Cabin Syrup—were transferred to the new agency. Overnight the increased billings established B&B, Inc. as one of the leaders in the agency field.

First order of business after incorporation was to staff up to meet the demands of the new accounts. Both Bowles and Hobler shared the view that an agency's creative work was its most important asset. Before the arrival of Hobler with his dowry of a half dozen accounts, Bowles had written most of the copy with the help of a couple of junior writers, one of whom was Henrietta Owens, a former *Time* researcher. When Bowles hired her, she warned him she didn't know anything about advertising. Bowles said, "I don't care, as long as you can *write*."

A New Team

A primary need, the partners agreed, was a top creative person who could relieve Bowles of some of the writing. After exhaustive screening—there were plenty of candidates available in those Depression days—they selected Walter O'Meara, a copywriter at J. Walter Thompson in Chicago whose ads Benton had spotted and admired. O'Meara, a big, handsome Minnesotan with a warm, winsome manner, was not only a crack copywriter, but an aspiring author as well. He eventually published several historical novels, mainly set in Minnesota where his father had been a logger.

A number of bright, talented people left old-line agencies to join what Benton's biographer Sidney Hyman called "the excitement at Benton & Bowles":

Urbane, efficient Jim Adams, formerly assistant to the president of Johns-Manville, became general manager. He left in 1939 to join Colgate, eventually became a senior partner of Lazard Frères.

Bill Baker—tall and darkly handsome—left BBDO to take over the account work on Maxwell House Coffee and Log Cabin Syrup, the beginning of a distinguished 33-year career with the agency. He became president in 1951 and chairman of the board in 1954.

Bob Lusk, affable, tall, soldier-straight (in later years he was

often mistaken for General George C. Marshall), the very image of
the agency president he was to become. Lusk came from R. H. Macy
where he'd been advertising director. Before that he had been an assistant account executive at the Blackman Company on Procter &
Gamble's Ivory Soap.*

And later, another pivotal—and painful—figure in B&B history, Ted Bates, whom Bowles had worked with at BBDO.

Others who joined the new team included copywriters Duane
Jones and Maitland Jones; ex-newspaperman Tom Revere, first as a
publicity writer, later as head of the radio department; Tom Carnese,
tough, scrappy, street-wise production chief; and two art directors to
share Jim Balch's workload, Walter Stocklin and Charlie Faldi. Faldi
eventually headed the art department, retiring in 1956.

With this infusion of new blood, Benton & Bowles went to
work on one of the biggest problems among the newly inherited accounts, an ailing Maxwell House Coffee.

Teddy Roosevelt, Sloganeer

Legend has it that Teddy Roosevelt, while enjoying a cup of
Maxwell House Coffee at the Nashville home of Joel Cheek, de-
veloper of the blend, first uttered the famous phrase, "Good to the
last drop!"

Whatever its origin, the slogan has been one of the most en-
during and valuable properties in advertising history. During the '20s
Maxwell House was the largest-selling brand of coffee in the country,
and by 1928 when General Foods bought the business, it sold some 50
million pounds a year. But in 1929, soon after the stock market crash,
Maxwell House Coffee's volume began to plummet, and by the time
B&B took over the account volume was down to 39 million pounds
and there was no joy in Hoboken.

The first campaign the agency recommended was based on

---

*It is interesting to note that all eight B&B presidents were, or are, six feet or over, except Benton
who was about 5'10". A former B&B executive (himself 5'10") offered this theory as an explana-
tion: "Tall men like tall men around them. They feel more comfortable with them than with shorter
men. They tend to favor, unconsciously, tall men in selecting, hiring, promoting. It's a case of
natural selection."

"coffee nerves"—and still there was no joy in Hoboken. The client was cool to the idea, and gloomily talked about putting all the budget into outdoor billboards—"a discouraging start in a new assignment," an early account man observed. When Hobler was asked by Butler and his associates, Marion Harper, Sr. and Jim Brownlee, if he really felt the campaign had a chance of reversing the brand's downward trend, Hobler said, in a burst of candor that was to become a B&B characteristic, "no," and told them why. "Maxwell House Coffee is losing . . . to competition," he said, "in the fundamental area of quality. . . . Unless we make improvements in quality, no amount of advertising can reverse the trend."

Having blown the agency's recommendation out of the water himself, Hobler went on to say there were other things wrong with the marketing picture, such as packaging and price. He promised to return with a new recommendation.

Consumer research, which had worked so well for Bowles in developing a campaign for Certo, was now put to the service of Maxwell House Coffee.*

The agency asked 1,000 housewives "What do you think is the best coffee on the market?" A remarkably high percentage—230 women—said "Maxwell House." Yet, of this number, only forty women said they were buying it. "Why?" the agency asked the non-buyers. "Because it costs too much."

Chet Bowles theorized that a large volume-small profit margin policy could be part of the solution to the Maxwell House problem. Before the Depression most packaged goods marketers maintained wide profit margins. But as the Depression deepened, the grocery chains—particularly A&P and Kroger—began pushing their private brands at reduced prices and pennies-per-unit profit, which made sharp inroads into the franchises of advertised brands. Bowles and Hobler thought Maxwell House Coffee should fight the chains on the price front.

---

*Bowles, a firm believer in the usefulness of opinion surveys in his advertising days, had little luck with them in his political career. On three occasions they played him false. In 1948, when he was running for governor of Connecticut, a poll predicted he "couldn't possibly win." (He won by a narrow margin.) In 1950 a poll showed he was "a shoo-in." (He lost by a wide margin.) When he was running for the nomination for governor in 1954, a poll showed he could win—but he failed to make the poll results known—and lost the nomination.

"A Startling Recommendation"

Hobler returned to GF in the fall of 1932 with what he called "the most startling recommendation I have ever known in advertising and marketing." He told Butler and his associates the agency recommended five actions for their beleaguered coffee brand:

Improve the blend so it would at least have parity with Chase & Sanborn, its chief competitor.

Vacuum pack the coffee. (Chase & Sanborn was selling "freshness.")

Cut the price 5 cents a pound.

Put all the advertising appropriation into *Showboat*, a one-hour variety show, developed by Bowles, which had an unprecedented weekly budget of $6,500. (Hobler was at first afraid to recommend such an outrageous budget to the client, but Bowles insisted.)

And, in order to pay for all this, reduce the advertising budget by $2 million dollars, from $3.1 million to $1.1 million.

The client was flabbergasted. "Put all our money in one radio show? Cut our profit to the bone? And, most flabbergasting of all, an agency actually suggesting we cut the advertising budget! You'll have to increase sales 20 percent," said the client, "just to break even." It was a big gamble, Hobler knew. A life or death gamble.

"We knew if sales didn't turn sharply upward," he wrote later, "Maxwell House Coffee and Benton & Bowles would be completely out of advertising by mid-year."

The client finally decided, despite the gamble, "it is our only chance." (Chase & Sanborn thought the Maxwell House people had flipped their coffee lids. "They've surrendered any chance for profit," they solemnly observed.)

Barely two months after the radical marketing strategy was launched and the price reduction announced on *Showboat* in January 1933, the sales rate of the brand not only passed the break-even point, but increased to an incredible 70–80 percent in the areas reached by the radio program.

Now there was joy in Hoboken! And kudos to the agency from everybody at GF from Colby Chester on down.

The Triangle of Marketing Success

The Maxwell House Coffee experience is a textbook example of what Hobler came to call "The Triangle of Marketing Success" (the title of his unpublished autobiography written, in part, by Doug Newton). Success in marketing, Hobler contended, could only be assured if these three legs of the triangle are in place:

Product quality—Equal or superior to your competition.

Merchandising—Packaging, price, promotion.

Advertising—An idea or a vehicle—such as *Showboat*—that projects the product story memorably.

Hobler first evolved the idea of the marketing triangle back in Illinois when he was selling manure spreaders and 4-gang plows. It would become the keystone of his advertising philosophy, and of the many marketing successes he would help to build for the agency's clients during the next third of a century.

"Ain't Dat Sumpin'?"

The instant success of *Showboat* and the dramatic turnaround of Maxwell House Coffee further strengthened B&B's relationship with its first and major client, and moved the agency into the big league in the burgeoning new medium of radio. Within the space of five years radio had grown from a cat's whisker-and-crystal novelty nobody knew quite what to do with, to a powerfully effective advertising medium. As early as 1925 H. V. Kaltenborn, before he became the doomsdayer of CBS, wrote in the *Brooklyn Eagle*, "Direct advertising has already been abandoned by most advertisers who have tried radio as a medium."

The idea of "sponsoring" a radio broadcast had its first tentative beginnings with discreet little "talks" by advertisers. A greeting card manufacturer offered a talk on the history of greeting cards; Gillette, a story of beards through the ages. Stations, anxious to preserve the dignity of the airwaves—and their franchise—forbade direct sell, and under no circumstances were prices to be mentioned. All this changed under the hammer blows of the Depression, when many local stations accepted meal tickets, farm produce and other barter items to stay alive. In what was perhaps the first example of radio censorship WEAF, the NBC station in New York, urged a vacuum cleaner company not to use the line, "Sweep no more, my lady," lest it offend lovers of "My Old Kentucky Home" (or, possibly, loathers of bad puns).

Bill Benton was an early convert to radio. While at Lord & Thomas, he had signed *Amos 'n' Andy* for Pepsodent and had seen the pioneer serial become a national addiction. This show, more than any other factor, boomed the sale of radio sets—totaling more than $800 million in 1929—and made radio a truly national medium. During the weekday from 7:00 to 7:15 p.m. virtually all intelligent life in the country ceased as millions gathered around their Atwater Kents to hear Andy remark, "Ain't dat sumpin'?" and learn about the latest doings of the Fresh Air Taxicab Company. Movie houses had to stop the picture for the nightly broadcast of the program; office hours were adjusted to allow people to get home and have supper before seven; and even the routine of the White House was interrupted so President Hoover could listen. In a grim, Depression-ridden time, the nation could forget its troubles for a while as it listened to radio's comedy and musical stars, many of them ex-vaudevillians: Eddie Cantor for Chase & Sanborn; Texaco Fire Chief Ed Wynn, the Perfect Fool; Jack Pearl as Baron Munchhausen; Stoopnagel and Budd; Jack Benny and Rudy Vallee. (President Hoover once told Vallee, "If you can sing a song that would make people forget the Depression, I'll give you a medal!")

Benton had little trouble selling Bowles on the power and potential of the new medium, and Bowles very quickly became a radio pro, both as a copywriter and as a creator of programs. The first radio show of the new agency was a series Bowles put together for Hellmann's featuring Morton Downey, "The Irish Thrush." (Downey, an incorrigible practical joker, once walked into a CBS studio where a sportscaster friend was on the air and proceeded, deadpan, to undress him, removing shoes, socks, shirt, trousers and underwear, while the sportscaster struggled bravely—and finally nakedly—to continue his broadcast.)

Another popular early B&B show was the Best Foods Boys, Billy Jones and Ernie Hare. They were also, at various times, the Happiness Boys for Happiness candy stores; the Taystee Loafers for the bread company; and the Interwoven Pair for Interwoven socks. This was the golden era of sponsor identification when every show had the advertiser's name in the title: the A&P Gypsies, the Gold Dust Twins, the Cliquot Club Eskimos.

Bowles later created the daytime serial *Young Dr. Malone* for General Foods and wrote the first episodes before turning it over to a team of writers, Frank Provo and John Pickard, who wrote it until the show was sold a few years later to Procter & Gamble. When Provo and Pickard learned that P&G had hired a new writing team and that they were out, they devised a devilish kind of swan song. Their last episode, broadcast on a Friday, centered on an automobile accident in which Dr. Malone, a neurosurgeon, lost his right arm. But by the following Monday, the new writing team had performed a miracle: the young doctor's arm had been restored, good as new!

"Come Aboard, Folks!"

It was a heady, exciting, freewheeling time for the "hot radio agency," as people in the industry were calling B&B. At first there was no formal radio production department—Bowles hated the idea of departments. Bowles produced, the writers produced, even Hobler jumped in and produced, greatly enjoying the role of impresario. "I don't think I've ever had as much pleasure in the agency business," he wrote, "as during those early years we worked with the wonderful people on our various shows." The medium was an undiscovered country, and the agency was exploring, inventing new techniques as it went along.

Showboat was the first program to have a live audience and, for better or worse, the first to use cue cards that read LAUGH or AP-PLAUD. It also was first to use integrated commercials. Before *Showboat*, an announcer just stood up before a microphone and read the commercial. Bowles conceived the idea of making commercials more real by having the actors actually drink coffee, rattle their cups and smack their lips in appreciation. The show itself had a "real" setting

—another first—a Mississippi River paddlewheel steamer which every week Cap'n Andy, played by Charles Winninger, docked at a different river town, with appropriate sound effects: blast of steam whistle, surge of water, clatter of the gangplank, as Tiny Ruffner, the announcer, called out, "Come aboard, folks! Your ticket of admission is just your loyalty to Maxwell House Coffee!"

Hobler wrote later that when *Showboat* "played" New Orleans, "there were 2,000 people waiting for Cap'n Andy on the dock!" When it was scheduled to "call" at Pittsburgh, a young General Foods salesman telegramed the home office for tickets. When they wired back SHOWBOAT MYTHICAL. NO TICKETS AVAILABLE, he got on the phone and said, "I don't know about that damned 'mythical' stuff, but I've got seventy people coming and I need those tickets!"

The Magic Formula Works Again

The highly visible success of *Showboat* also attracted considerable attention from other advertisers. By the end of 1934 the agency had a new blue-chip account—Colgate, for four products; it also was assigned by Bristol Myers to handle radio production of Ipana on a fee basis.

Colgate president Bayard Colgate, a good friend of Benton's, had "brought the nose of Benton & Bowles into the tent" by recommending the agency to Ed Little, Colgate's colorful executive vice-president and sales manager. The first assignment was Cashmere Bouquet, soon followed by Palmolive Shave Cream, Supersuds and Palmolive Soap, which, like Maxwell House Coffee, was suffering a decline in sales. Applying the same formula that got Maxwell House Coffee perking again, the agency recommended cutting the price to 5 cents a bar, reducing the advertising budget from $4 million to $1.6 million, and putting most of the budget into a radio show Bowles had developed, *Palmolive Beauty Box.*

Again the magic worked. By the end of the year, sales had increased from 600,000 cases to 1.1 million, and company profits were up nearly $2 million.

"It's Town Hall Tonight!"

Out of budgetary necessity, the agency invented another historic first in radio. Fred Allen had a half hour show sponsored by Best Foods which was not going to be renewed. Initially, the plan was to switch sponsorship to Sal Hepatica and expand the program to a full hour. But this was too rich for Sal Hepatica's blood, so the agency recommended that Sal Hepatica and Ipana jointly sponsor the hour.

Lee Bristol of Bristol Myers was dubious. "*Two* products on one show? What would happen to sponsor identification? (Until then a sacred cow of radio.) Do you have any examples where two products were successfully sold on the same program?" All the agency could think of, wrote Chet Dudley, an account man at the time, was a couple of "weak daytime cooking school monologists."

Bristol finally bought the idea and the first dual product sponsorship (and the harbinger of "clutter") made its debut in the fall of 1934 on *Town Hall Tonight*. The show also featured the first integrated product line: "Ipana for the Smile of Beauty. Sal Hepatica for the Smile of Health." The line, used successfully for many years, was written by Bowles who surrounded the slogan with a musical phrase, thus creating what may have been the first musical jingle.

Fred Allen was a very funny man, both on the air and off, and one of the few radio comedians who could ad lib. In an early exchange between him and Jack Benny—who reputedly was not an ad libber—Allen got off a particularly acid insult, to which Benny replied, "You wouldn't get away with that if my writers were here!" which, come to think of it, wasn't a bad ad lib.

"Aunt Mabel" Claflin, the longtime receptionist on the ninth floor of 444 Madison—where the agency moved in July, 1932—once had a distinguished visitor. He looked familiar to her, but the name he gave her—Derf Nella—was not. Only when Hobler came out to greet the visitor did she discover it was Fred Allen.

Within a short time *Town Hall Tonight* was number three among network shows. With *Showboat* first and *Palmolive Beauty Box* second, and with more than 60 percent of its billing in radio, B&B by the mid-'30s was unquestionably the Old Pro of the medium.

Good News and Bad News

The radio marriage of Ipana and Sal Hepatica was so successful the agency decided to ask Bristol for the entire Ipana account. (It rankled a little to see Ipana's agency, Pedlar & Ryan, reaping the billings of a B&B-produced show.) But two weeks before the solicitation, the agency got some good news and some bad news.

The good news was that Ed Little had awarded B&B the complete line of Colgate's drug products, including Colgate Dental Cream.

The bad news was that the agency had to resign Ipana and the other Bristol Myers products, which meant giving up the *Fred Allen Show.* (It went to Young & Rubicam.) The agency tried to hang onto both toothpastes, even setting up a separate two-man group, but the conflict was unacceptable to both clients. For a time it looked as though it might work. If it had, perhaps the long history of product conflicts—a chronic agency bugaboo—would have been different.

"The Firm Will Fall Apart!"

In a recent interview, Chet Bowles said, "Bill was always trying to develop an alternative to Benton & Bowles."

Late in 1933, soon after B&B acquired the Colgate business, Benton first announced to his two partners that he wanted to leave the agency. At first they didn't take him seriously. "Hobe and I didn't think you would leave," Bowles later wrote to Benton. "I'm sure Hobe had no real idea you had any such plan. He had a strong suspicion, in fact, that what you really wanted was a larger share of the business."

But Benton was serious, although complications postponed his plans for more than a year. One complication was the unsettling effect his announcement had on his associates. Both Bowles and Hobler protested that "the firm will fall apart." Other key people felt uneasy about their personal future without Benton at the helm.

Another complication was the reaction of Colgate. Ed Little "was damned mad about it," Jim Rogers, an assistant to Bowles at the time, recalled recently. Little said he'd given the agency his business with the understanding that Benton would supervise it. Hobler wrote later, "I was not happy about this turn of events."* He felt that Benton had been less than candid in not saying anything about his retirement plans when Ed Little assigned the Colgate business to B&B.

In the face of these adverse reactions, Benton agreed to stay on for a while, and work on a new campaign for Colgate Dental Cream. The idea for the campaign was Hobler's: that toothpaste combatted bad breath. The theme eventually developed—that Colgate not only cleans your teeth but freshens your breath—was to run for many years and help make Colgate the leading toothpaste until Crest, a later B&B assignment from Procter & Gamble, toppled it in the early '60s.

Benton Leaves

The first step in the final parting between Benton and the agency he cofounded came December 30, 1935, when he turned back all his stock to the firm. Benton and his wife, Helen, had taken an extended vacation in Europe the previous spring, and contrary to people's fears, the agency hadn't fallen apart. In the spring of 1936 the Bentons went to Nassau for two months, and still the agency remained afloat. On April 1—his 36th birthday—Benton formally resigned, "in order," the press release said, "to devote his energies to interests outside the advertising field." The release also announced these management changes: Bowles became chairman of the board, Hobler president. Walter O'Meara, Jim Adams, Ted Bates, Bob Lusk and Bill Baker remained vice-presidents.

The $1,000,000 Legend

The popular belief that both Benton and Bowles left advertising with a million dollars each is at least partly true. Benton's accumulated assets did, in fact, eventually amount to around a million (he realized $250,000 in 1935 alone). Bowles, when he left in 1941,

---

*Other reports of the time indicate that Hobler was more than "not happy," that there were many heated exchanges between him and Benton on the subject of his leaving.

realized less—about $600,000. Benton's stock sale was arranged by a brilliant young Manhattan-born lawyer, A. M. Gilbert, of the law firm of Davis & Gilbert, which had just been retained as the agency's counselors for a fee of $5,000 a year. The rather unusual severance arrangement is described in Benton's biography:

> Benton's stock was divided into six equal blocks. Payments would be made in six annual installments . . . with the price of each block to be five times the average earnings on the same amount of stock during the previous three years. If the firm disintegrated, Benton's return would be negligible. Only if the firm prospered would he receive a high return.

As it developed, the agency did prosper, and Benton eventually did realize the much publicized million.

The Boys Were Doing All Right

The agency's ability to continue successfully after its dynamic cofounder had left was due to the caliber of its people, its extraordinary success in radio, and the steadfastness of its clients. By the end of 1935 it had a creative staff that was the envy of the industry, attracting the hottest talent around. (Sinclair Lewis once applied for a $100-a-week copywriting job, but Bowles was afraid the author of *Main Street* was just looking for material for a satirization of Madison Avenue.) Walter O'Meara, creative director, was the kind of boss who did a lot of writing himself. He and Bowles wrote much of the copy, including highly successful comic strip ads for Post Toasties, Raisin Bran and other GF products.* (O'Meara went on to become one of the highest paid copywriters in the country.**) The radio department, which Bowles finally conceded was needed, wrote and produced more than a dozen programs, including the three top-

---

*Bowles is credited with making the first use in advertising of comic strips, or "doghouse" strips, so called because the archetypal strip had a picture of a man who'd been consigned by his wife to a real doghouse. The comic strip ad was the spiritual (if that is the word) forerunner of the slice-of-life TV commercial.

**Probably the two highest paid copywriters in advertising's history were John F. Kennedy, who often took a percentage of the sales his copy produced (one year, in the early 1900s, his take was $500,000 from a Liquozone ad); and Claude C. Hopkins, whose salary at Lord & Thomas was $185,000 a year.

rated daytime series, *When a Girl Marries*, *Portia Faces Life* and *Young Dr. Malone* (before he lost and regained his arm).

Account management had impressive strength: Hobler on General Foods; Bowles, who by now had turned over much of the writing to O'Meara and his staff and had taken over some of Benton's client responsibilities; Ted Bates, top contact man on Colgate; Bob Lusk and Bill Baker.

Most encouraging of all, the agency's clients stood fast, even Colgate (the final chapter of that relationship was yet to be written). By year's end, they numbered seven: General Foods, Best Foods, Colgate, Standard Milling, Ballentine, Drake's Cakes and Eastern Airline (then owned by General Motors), which stayed with the agency just eight months—seven months longer than it tarried in 1965.

It was a watershed year for the agency, a time of some inner turmoil and regrouping. If there was concern for the future, there was also confidence, a confidence buttressed by the agency's record billings—nearly $10 million in 1935—which placed it sixth among U.S. agencies, and record profits.

"Chet," Benton wrote his mother, "is having a new schooner built." Hobler, who always liked to live well (he had a chauffeur-driven Cadillac as early as the St. Louis days), "is buying a new yacht," and Benton himself had "put in a swimming pool and a billiard table near the tennis courts" at his country place.

The boys were doing all right.

So well, in fact, that the partners decided to share some of the goodies with their associates in the first distribution of stock to employees in the advertising industry. Gilbert—"Gil," as he would be called by everyone at B&B for the next 35 years—wrote the contracts, and the company's first ledger records the transfer of about 3,000 shares to several executives. (The name of Jim Balch, the man with the drunken desk, was listed, but crossed out.)

When Milton Biow heard of the stock distribution, he said to Hobler, "You're taking money out of your own pocket. What are you trying to do, give away the business?"

Long after Milton Biow, the man and the agency, had passed

from the advertising scene, Benton & Bowles was still "giving away the business" to members of its corporate family—in 1978 there were more than 300 stock holders—and still prospering.

Three
Chet & Hobe
1936–41

"Clients sometimes ask me," David Ogilvy wrote some years ago, "what would become of our agency if I were run over by a taxicab. . . . J. Walter Thompson survived the departure of Mr. Thompson . . . the retirement of Raymond Rubicam failed to arrest the progress of Young & Rubicam. . . . When Benton and Bowles left their agency it changed—for the better."

Probably no man is indispensable to the success of a business, even an extraordinary mover and shaker like Bill Benton. But for the first few months after he left to begin a long association with his old friend Robert Maynard Hutchins, president of the University of Chicago, the agency "ran into some difficulties," as an early, unpublished history of the agency by Chet Dudley described it, "particularly with new business prospects who asked 'Is Benton & Bowles going to split?' "

One reverse the agency suffered had nothing to do with Benton's departure: the loss of Bristol Myers because of the conflict with Colgate. (As an account man then with the agency remarked on the situation, "The Lord thy God is a jealous God.") To offset this drop in billings, Bowles and Bates aggressively pressed the quest for new business, particularly that of Continental Baking where both of them had close contacts since their work on the account at BBDO. A point Bowles made in new business presentations was the youth of the agency—the average age of executives at the time was 32.

With much of his time spent on account solicitation, Bowles decided in the summer of 1936 that he needed an assistant to replace Jim Rogers who had left to join Lord & Thomas. A full-page ad in *Printer's Ink* drew 200 letters, one of which was from a 26-year-old Bowdoin College dropout and sometime drummer with a dance band,

Louis Thornton Steele. Steele—"Ted," as he liked to be called after his idol, Ted Lewis—at the time was with Louis Glaser, Inc., a small Boston agency. He wrote a 16-page letter, followed it with a telegram, then pestered Bowles's secretary by telephone until Bowles saw him and hired him, not as an assistant, but as a recruit in the research department.

"Hatching Germs"

Thus began a 37-year career with the agency that saw Steele move progressively from research to account work, to radio (and later TV) programming, to account management, to executive vice-president, to the agency's international operation, to chairman of the board, and finally to chairman of the executive committee.

But it was with Dr. Lyman D. Chalkely, dignified academic head of research, that Steele began, one of a staff of about fifteen which included an obscure writer of research reports, Adolph Toigo (later head of Lennen & Newell, a leading agency for many years until it went bankrupt in 1972).

"We were working on Supersuds," Steele recalls, "which had the claim, 'Supersuds gets clothes hospital clean.' I remember all of us in research sat around on covered Pyrex pie plates full of germs to prove that bacteria were incubated by body heat."

The push for new business by Bowles and Bates finally bore fruit. On January 1, 1937, after toasting the new year the night before, they learned that the agency had been awarded the Continental business, an occasion for drinking more toasts which, if they did, may have been followed by generous potions of Eno Effervescent Salt, a small account secured a few months before.

With the repeal of Prohibition, distillers were another source of new accounts, although the agency was "very suspicious of whiskey business," Dudley wrote, adding with a straight face, "It seemed as though there would be a lot of headaches in it." Reason for Dudley's concern: Many liquor companies "were not properly set up with the right kind of sales and advertising people."

One company the agency solicited was an exception: Calvert

Distilleries, headed by an experienced marketing man, a former sales manager of Loose-Wiles Biscuit Company, whom Hobler had known in St. Louis. In the spring of 1937 Calvert assigned the agency four whiskies which were to be supervised by the man who helped land the business, Zenus L. Potter, who Ted Steele said "looked like a Roman senator."* Steele, weary of hatching germs in the research department, became the Calvert assistant account executive.

"I damned near got lynched on one of my first assignments on the account," Steele remembers. "A photographer and I were down at a race track in Kentucky taking pictures for a campaign for Kentucky Pride. As the horses rounded the final turn, I said to the photographer, 'Get a real good head-on shot.' So he got right out on the track. With the horses practically on top of him, he took the picture. The flash bulb went off, the horse in the lead—the favorite—shied, the others piled up in ghastly confusion, and the crowd was ready to riot. We just made it out the gate ahead of them."

Old Drum was another Calvert product, a bottom-of-the-line bourbon whose label pictured a broken snare drum with the line, "It Can't Be Beat." For ex-drummer Steele, Old Drum was a natural assignment, as fortuitous a bit of type-casting as one is likely to find.

"We had miniature gold drums made up," he said, "and I presented them to drummers with the big bands of the period—Fred Waring, Horace Heidt and His Musical Knights, Russ Morgan, but, unfortunately, not Ina Ray Hutton's All Girl Orchestra—no women could be associated with liquor advertising."

Bill Tompkins, 42-year veteran of B&B and head of the art studio for 25 years, has a vivid recollection of Old Drum.

"We had a case of half-pints in the studio," he said, "but nobody touched the stuff because the rumor was it was such rot gut you'd go blind if you drank it. One night we're working late—we sometimes worked all night in those days—and Vinnie Smythe decided, what the hell, he'd take a chance. So he opens a bottle, takes a few swigs and flops down on the couch in the foyer for a nap. While he's asleep, I paint the lens of his glasses with lamp black. When

---

*It was customary then, and for many years after, for the "new business department" to go out of business once a new account had been won, with the man who had made the presentation being assigned to the new acquisition.

Vinnie wakes up, he struggles to his feet, blinking and shouting, 'My God, I've gone blind!' " (A prank worthy of Jim Balch who, by this time, had died of a liver ailment.)

In Tompkins's early days, advertising made extensive use of famous artists: Howard Chandler Christie; Raleigh, who did a series of American scenes for Maxwell House Coffee; Gustav Tengren; Felix Schmidt; H.T. Webster, the "Life's Darkest Moments" cartoonist, who did a series for Post Toasties; Rockwell Kent and Norman Rockwell.

"There was a terrible mixup on artists once," Tompkins recalls. "The account people on Bituminous Coal signed up Norman Rockwell for some institutional ads. The first picture arrives in a big packing case, and Charlie Faldi and I unwrap it. We take one look and Charlie says, 'Nail it back up.' The painting wasn't by Norman Rockwell, it was by Rockwell Kent! The dumb guys had signed up the wrong Rockwell. Problem was, Kent couldn't draw the human figure. The picture was of a kid in a hospital bed—if you stood him up, he'd have been nine feet tall! Harold Cressingham, an artist on staff, had to redo the whole thing."*

Lou Gehrig Strikes Out

By now radio, not print, was king, accounting for more than 60 percent of the agency's billings in 1937. Among the new shows that year: *The Kate Smith Hour* ("When the Moon Comes Over the Mountain") for Swans Down Cake Flour, and Joe ("Wanna Buy a Duck?") Penner for Huskies, a new GF cereal named by Fred Bell, an account man who received $25 for the idea. Kate and Joe appeared as comic strip characters in the first tune-in ads promoting the shows.

Huskies also sponsored a second show, Ripley's *Believe It Or Not*, which once featured Yankee star Lou Gehrig, the Iron Man of Baseball, in a testimonial, and which led to one of radio's famous

---

*Norman Rockwell was used for an early Maxwell House Coffee ad: a picture of two old southern colonels relaxing over a cup of coffee and a game of checkers, and at the bottom "Maxwell House Coffee—Good to the Last Drop." When Bowles saw the ad, he added the line: "You know, Henry, you're an old fool about everything except coffee." Both versions were tested; the one with Bowles's line scored three times higher than the other one.

gaffes. The commercial dialogue between announcer Ford Bond and Lou Gehrig went something like this:

GEHRIG: I start off with some fruit . . .
            then I dive into a bowl of
            Wheaties.

            (LONG PAUSE WHILE PEOPLE IN
            CONTROL ROOM GO CRAZY)

BOND: (RECOVERING) Ah—Lou, I
            thought you always ate
            HUSKIES.

            (ANOTHER LONG PAUSE WHILE
            GEHRIG THINKS THIS OVER)

GEHRIG: That's right, Ford, I always
            eat HUSKIES.

But the damage had been done. The hated name of the competitor's product had gone out to millions of homes, and there was no calling it back.

"I lived in agony all weekend after it happened," recalls Frank Smith, Huskies brand manager at the time (who would join B&B a few years later). "Ralph Butler (GF advertising director) didn't like the idea of athletes endorsing his products in the first place."

The wire services carried the story, the *New York World Telegram* ran a picture and story, and for weeks GF salesmen were greeted by store managers with a cheery "Hi, Lou," "Hi, Mr. Gehrig." Gehrig returned his check for the commercial to General Foods, they sent it back to him, and *that* got wide coverage. The publicity was invaluable, but ultimately it didn't help. In 1942 Huskies joined the ghostly legion of new products that don't make it in the market place.

It's hard today to imagine a minor incident evoking such public response—until one remembers Orsen Welles's "War of the Worlds" broadcast a couple of years later. Radio had a pervasive in-

fluence which would only be exceeded a decade later by the even more
pervasive influence of television.

Westward Ho!

With *Showboat* riding the crest—after a year on the air it had
a 45 rating and consistently topped Rudy Vallee's *Fleishmann Hour*
—the agency moved the show to the West Coast to be closer to its
source of guest stars. There it was produced out of the agency's newly
opened production office which during the next several years also
handled such history-making radio programs as *Good News*, *Burns
and Allen*, and the *Fanny Brice (Baby Snooks)—Frank Morgan Show*.

Still feeling in an expansive mood, the agency opened Benton
& Bowles-Chicago in the fall of 1937, with Stuart Sherman as president and Edward Aleshire and Arthur Marquette as vice-presidents.
Bowles had tried to hire Aleshire, who was copy chief of Lord &
Thomas, and Sherman, vice-president for sales at Pepsodent, but
neither wanted to leave Chicago. So B&B went to Chicago, an experiment in expansion that had only modest, brief success. Two years
later Sherman and Marquette told the folks back in New York they
wanted to go it alone, and set up their own agency, which flourished
in Chicago and New York for several years. (Not until 36 years later
would B&B venture into the Windy City again. In May 1975 it
opened its second Chicago office with Dale Landsman as general
manager.)

With the influx of new business and increased appropriations
from existing clients, the agency's billings soared to $15 million in
1937, up 53 percent from 1936. To help handle the new business, the
agency added a heavyweight: Clarence Goshorn, brilliant, ebullient
University of Michigan professor of rhetoric turned advertising man,
whom Hobler had worked with at Erwin, Wasey.

Having moved out of the shallows of the early years into safer
waters, B&B took stock of itself to see what kind of an agency it had
become, and what made it different from its competitors. In the history prepared by Dudley, it concluded that, "five of the present six
leaders are approaching the job of advertising along . . . similar lines,"

placing major emphasis on "the creative end of the business . . . Young & Rubicam, J. Walter Thompson, Ruthrauf & Ryan, Blackett-Sample & Hummert and Benton & Bowles." How did B&B see itself as different from the others? "Our contact work . . . is not spread out over a long list of clients . . . we have only six . . . the others have thirty or more. . . . We handle only low-cost, big-volume units, none of which cost more than $1.50 . . . we are not cluttered up with any automobile or 'gadget' accounts . . . (and) our accounts each bill a million or more."

To underscore how mature and professional the agency had become, Dudley added, "No longer is it necessary for Mr. Bowles and Mr. O'Meara to ask the art director to make layouts over and over again . . . no longer is it necessary for Mr. Hobler to go over all the plans in detail before a client meeting." (Author's note: Remembering Hobe, I'll bet he still did.)

The new prosperity, and a developing concern about taking care of its "family," brought another benefit to the agency's employees. On November 18, 1937, the board of directors approved a group insurance plan, prepared by A. M. Gilbert, the first in the advertising industry, which gave all employees—there were 298—coverage equal to their annual salary up to $10,000.

"How to Succeed in Business Without Really Trying"

Even the $15-a-week mailroom boys were covered, although with salaries of less than $1,000 a year it could hardly be said that the survivors would be fixed for life. A gentle, forebearing man named Ed Holland was in charge of the mailroom, traditional training ground—before anyone thought of the Wharton School and the Harvard School of Business—of future account executives, media and research people, even copywriters. In the mailroom's heyday—mid-'30s to mid-'50s—Holland had as many as twenty young men at a time, many graduates of Yale, Harvard, Princeton and other Ivy League colleges, which at that time spawned a good share of the advertising industry's future executives.

Holland's boys were a mixed bag, and contributed their share to the folklore of the agency.

Tall, energetic Gil Stender used to sit in a fenced-in area outside general manager Jim Adams's office, Helen Scofield recalls. "Everytime Adams came out of his office," she says, "Gil would spring up and leap over the railing, hellbent on some errand, just to show he was on the ball." His agility paid off; he became head of traffic, and later vice-president and account supervisor on the Norwich Pharmacal Company account.*

Holland recalls sending one of his boys to Newark, a few minutes from New York on the Pennsylvania Railroad, telling him to "get off at Broad Street." The man got off at Broad Street, all right. But it was Broad Street in Philadelphia, a hundred miles away.

Helen Scofield remembers another mailroom boy, a wealthy scion with an independent income. "He used to sit at the bar in the Yale Club and hire a Western Union messenger to make his deliveries."

A former mailroom boy recalls that one of his duties was to go out every two hours during the day and move the Packard roadster belonging to the girl friend of a client, who worked as a receptionist at the agency.

Among Holland's alumni** were at least two agency presidents, several vice-presidents and senior vice-presidents, and a best-selling novelist. Esty Stowell, after leaving B&B as executive vice-president, became president of Olgivy & Mather; Bart Cummings graduated to Compton where he eventually became president and chairman of the board. (In 1979 he was elected to the Advertising Hall of Fame.) Bern Kanner is a group executive and director of Benton & Bowles International; Bill Schneider, now retired, was vice-president and director of business affairs; Irwin Siegelstein is executive vice-president for broadcasting at NBC; Don Wallace, a former executive producer, now owns decorating stores in Westchester County.

---

*On his 35th anniversary, the client honored Stender with a "Gil Stender Day" in Norwich, New York (pop. 10,000) with all the small-town trimmings: banners across the street, free beer and a parade led by the Norwich High School band.

**Ed Holland's boys always called him "Boss," even after they had become bosses themselves in various departments of the agency.

The best-selling novelist is Ed (Shepherd) Mead, author of several comic novels, including *How to Succeed in Business Without Really Trying* which Abe Burrows turned into a Broadway musical hit. Mead began writing for Floyd Gibbons's *Your True Adventure*, sponsored by Gillette, while still in the mailroom, and eventually headed the radio-TV copy department. *How to Succeed in Business Without Really Trying* is based, Mead says, on office politics he observed while with B&B, and was written in his office mornings before 9:15, an extracurricular activity some people resented. "He's sitting in there writing a *book!*" complained one account man. "Why isn't he working on my commercials?" With his book on the best-seller list,* Mead quit advertising and moved with his wife Annabel and children to Europe. He now lives and writes in London, and only occasionally dreams of shaving Bill Benton's Ediphone cylinders.

The Calm Before the Storm

The three-year period from the end of 1937 to the end of 1940 was relatively calm, without major crises. The agency had fully adapted to the absence of Benton, although the staff saw him occasionally when he was in town for board meetings. (He remained on the board until 1943 and maintained an office in the agency until then.) He traveled extensively in Europe during this period and, always interested in international affairs, made it a point to see and talk to top government officials in the countries he visited. Just back from a trip in 1938, Benton one day rushed excitedly into Hobler's office.

"Hobe," he said, "I've just seen Hitler and Mussolini. Have lunch with me and I'll tell you all about it."

Hobe looked up from a pile of layouts on his desk and said, "Can't today, Bill. Got to go over these whiskey ads for a client meeting."

There was little sense of impending disaster—either worldwide

---

*At one time in 1952, two books by B&B people were on *The New York Times* best-seller list. The other one was *White Collar Zoo*, by art director Clare Barnes.

or corporate—in the offices at 444 Madison. Billings remained, during the three-year period, at about the same $15-million level. A few new accounts were added: Hudnut-DuBarry, Prudential Life Insurance, Columbia Records and Dr. Pepper (years before its big national expansion). Jim Adams had taken over account responsibility on Colgate from Benton, with Ted Bates doing most of the day-to-day contact work. Ed Little, now president and chief executive of the Colgate Company, had seemingly accepted the departure of Benton which he had so strongly resisted, and resented, at the outset.

Then, suddenly, Jim Adams left to become executive vice-president of Colgate. Hobler described the situation: "The supervision of the Colgate account increasingly devolved on Ted Bates. Although Ed Little continued to have confidence in the work B&B was doing. . . . I suspect Little may have resented the fact that Bill Benton was no longer . . . supervising his business. The fruition of this situation was not long in coming."

"We'll Never be Able to Rebuild. . . ."

Occasionally there are eyewitnesses to crucial events of the past who can recreate the event in all its "I Was There" clarity. There are no known witnesses of the banishment of Hagar, or of the fall of Troy, but there are at least two living witnesses of the meetings on October 1, 1940, the day Hobler learned Ted Bates was pulling out of the agency, taking with him the $7-million Colgate account—half the agency's billings—and setting up his own agency. Jim Rogers, who had rejoined the agency in 1938 as general manager, describes the first meeting:

> We were called into Hobe's office—Chet Bowles, Bob Lusk, Bill Baker, probably Clarence Goshorn, the financial guy, Ralph Neuman, and me. Hobe was stretched out on the little love seat he had in his alcove, his head hung over the edge, saying, "This is the end, we'll never be able to rebuild the agency." Chet was saying, "Oh, snap out of it, Hobe. Of course we will. With our record on Colgate we can talk to Lever Brothers and Procter & Gamble." But Hobe was not to be consoled.

Later in the day, there was another meeting, in Clarence

Goshorn's office, which "Gil" Gilbert attended and recently described:

> Hobe said, "What do we do?" He was for liquidating the business—he was the kind of guy who couldn't stand failure. There was discussion by everybody, and the general consensus was to do it. Then I put in my two cents worth. "Hobe," I said, "you shouldn't do it. You should stay in business." Hobe looked up at me with tears in his eyes and said, "Gil, I thought you were a friend of mine." I told him I was, that's why I said what I did.

After the shock and pain had worn off, Hobler became his usual "take charge" self again. He asked Ralph Neuman to prepare contingency financial plans based on billings of $7 million, $6 million, down to $4 million. He called a meeting of top people and asked them to take a temporary cut in salary of 10 to 15 percent (reinstated ten months later), and told them that there would be no Christmas bonus.*

The defection didn't stop with Bates. Several key B&B people joined the new agency: copywriters (one was a talented young "comer," Rosser Reeves), account men, media and research specialists, radio department head Tom Revere and production head Tom Carnese. A few months later, Bob Lusk was persuaded by Ed Little to leave and join Bates to handle his Colgate account. There was one more defection: Continental Baking, which had followed Bates to B&B in 1936, now faithfully followed him to his new shop.

Gilbert, counselor and confidant of Hobler for most of his B&B career, said later, "Ed Little never really forgave Benton for leaving. He was just biding his time until Bates was ready to move. It took a long time for the chickens to come home to roost, but they finally did."

Jim Rogers attributes the Colgate loss, in part, to Bates's unhappiness. "The agency was paying off Benton," Rogers said recently, "Bowles was out of the office a lot of the time—he was already thinking about getting out of advertising himself. Bates figured,

---

*Everybody went along with the belt-tightening, but not everybody was happy about it. Tom Revere led his radio department through the halls singing:
"Hark, the herald angels sing,
We didn't get a goddam thing!"

'Why should I support these guys while I'm doing most of the work?' "

Whatever the reason (or reasons) for the loss, Hobler saw the misfortune as "a good lesson." The agency, he said, didn't have "the rapport and understanding with the client we should have had. Because we failed in this . . . I feel we got what was coming to us."

It was a lesson Hobler never forgot. No man was ever more conscientious thereafter in keeping his finger on the pulse of the client. One of his favorite dictums was, "Take care of the client's business and the client will take care of you."

"A New Era"

A month after the Bates/Colgate debacle—when those left behind could look at each other without crying—Chet Bowles wrote a letter to Procter & Gamble. Neil McElroy, then head of the P&G brand operation, and his assistant Howard Morgens (both later would become successively president, then chairman of the board), invited the agency to visit them. Shortly after the visit, on July 1, 1941, the big Cincinnati soap-maker awarded Ivory Snow to Benton & Bowles, the first of what were to be many assignments. Bowles announced the good news in a memorandum to the organization: "Procter & Gamble is one of the three or four most desirable clients in the country. The . . . organization is capable and aggressive. And perhaps just as important, they are the kind of people with whom it is always pleasant and stimulating to work."

The assignment began a new era for the agency. As the association matured, B&B came to know at first hand the unique character of their new client, which *Dun's Review* in 1963 named America's Number One marketer. "Thoroughness lies at the heart of the Procter & Gamble character," a former executive vice-president once said. "It constantly cuts across all other of the company's characteristics." Benton & Bowles came to know, too, that a special quality marked the client—agency relationship; that, as one observer said, "Their integrity and fairness permeate every dimension of what they do."

The quality and character of its clients inevitably shape the quality and character of an advertising agency. Perhaps more than any other single influence, the 35-year association with Procter & Gamble has shaped the development of the agency and, by its discipline, its scrupulous standards, its expectation of excellence, has helped give Benton & Bowles the lineaments of a truly modern agency.

But all that was in the future—a future that almost didn't happen.

After six months of "handling the Ivory Snow account," Hobler wrote, "we almost lost it."

The problem: The agency was trying to give the new client a lesson in how to sell soap which, with this knowing advertiser, was like trying to teach your grandmother to suck eggs. The disagreement centered on a media recommendation. The agency had recommended a nightime radio show, *Junior Miss*, with Shirley Temple. Procter & Gamble, virtual inventor of the soap opera, thought a daytime serial would better suit its needs.

It soon came to a head.

Clarence Goshorn happened to meet Neil McElroy on the street in New York and stopped to chat. "You know, Clarence," McElroy said, "we're not as happy with Benton & Bowles as we'd like to be."

Goshorn, alarmed, urged McElroy to come back to the agency with him to talk to Hobler. Hobler told McElroy that he would take over complete management supervision of the brand, and asked him to give B&B eight months to see "if this agency is right for Ivory Snow and Procter & Gamble," adding that if "things work out for Ivory Snow . . . we would like to think . . . you will give us additional Procter & Gamble assignments."

Not quite eight months later, Morgens called on the agency to say that they now considered Benton & Bowles "right for Procter & Gamble," gave the agency two more products (Chipso and Naphtha Soap), and promised a new product assignment that he confidentially told Hobler "stands a good chance of revolutionizing the entire soap industry."

Mr. Ivory Snow

The man who in eight months was able to straighten out Ivory Snow and make Benton & Bowles "right for Procter & Gamble" was Frank Smith, a former art director who switched to brand and account work because, as he says, "I couldn't draw well enough." A merry, ruddy-faced, slightly rotund man with blue eyes and a halo of white hair, Frank is probably the only agency man to (1) be called "beloved" by a client; and (2) come to blows (almost) with the same client and still remain on the account. (The fight was over Ivory Snow's marketing strategy, a subject Frank Smith could be extremely passionate about.)*

Before coming to B&B and taking over responsibility for Ivory Snow, Smith was a client himself—a brand man at General Foods on various cereals, including Grape-Nuts. (In 1931 the brand sponsored the Admiral Byrd broadcasts from the North Pole where, it is said, the Admiral and his party not only ate the cereal, but used it for traction under the wheels of their plane.) He joined the agency in June 1941, and for the next 27 years—with his famous little fact book of marketing data always at hand—he guided the destinies of Ivory Snow, the longest service on a brand in P&G's and B&B's history. During this long tenure, he skillfully deployed the soap product against a formidable field of competitors, and saw it not only survive in a world of detergents, but prosper, the only laundry soap that did. By promoting the product for baby wash and by using Gift Pax that were distributed to new mothers in hospitals—among other advertising and merchandising efforts—Ivory Snow's business doubled in 1950, and increased steadily for the next seven years. During the years of commuting to Cincinnati—always by overnight sleeper until the service was discontinued—Smith worked with no fewer than 29 brand managers. Hobler once asked the client, "Why so many changes on Ivory

---

*The man Smith had the fight with was Morgan Hunter, now president of Scott Paper Company.

Snow?" He was told confidentially that the company depended on Frank Smith to teach their new brand men the rudiments of the business.

Fulsome praise is the common idiom of anniversary greetings, but in the case of Frank Smith the words of the organization memo from Hobler marking his 25th anniversary have a ring of sincerity, which anyone who knows him cannot deny: "I know of no man . . . who is so generally loved and respected by both coworkers and clients. . . . Frank should get the major portion of the credit for our development with Procter & Gamble."

Frank Smith retired in 1969 and lives with his wife Fritz in a historic pre-Revolutionary house in Scarsdale, surrounded by his collection of American antiques.

"I knew . . . I would never return to the business world. . . ."

December 7, 1941, was the end of a lot of things in America —the end of its isolation, the end of a kind of guilt-ridden peace. Like many Americans who hated war, Chet Bowles had been a noninterventionist. He had even written speeches for Charles Lindbergh, at the time a prominent member of the conservative isolationist group America First.

But all that changed with the Japanese attack on Pearl Harbor.

The day following the attack, Bowles called Hobler to tell him he had accepted the job of Connecticut State Ration Administrator. *The New York Times* carried a small item in its financial section that said Bowles had "received a leave of absence from six weeks to three months from Benton & Bowles to set up a statewide rationing system in Connecticut. His first duty will be the allotment of tires."

Bowles had first thought of leaving advertising in 1935, but Benton's departure had forced him to postpone his plans. Sometime later he had considered buying a daily newspaper in Connecticut, but shelved this plan when Bates left. Now world events had forced a decision. He described his feelings in his autobiography: "I knew even then that I would never return to the business world. It had treated me well, but my personal interests were elsewhere, and . . . I had finally cut the Gordian knot, or more accurately, it had been cut for me."

Gilbert drew up a stock sales plan for Bowles similar to Benton's, the proceeds to be paid to him over a period of years, based on agency earnings.

Another era in the life of the agency had ended. Both of the original partners had left to take up other careers, leaving Atherton Hobler as president and major stockholder. Having weathered the first real reversal in his business career, Hobler determinedly set about to do what he once thought couldn't be done—rebuild the agency to its previous strength.

Despite a promising beginning with a prestigious new client, it wouldn't be easy in a time of war.

Four

The War Years
1942–45

*A*t a Best Foods Christmas luncheon at which he was the speaker, Clarence Goshorn had trouble getting the group to come to order. He tinkled a spoon against his glass, began a few times with "Ladies and gentlemen. . .," but drinks had put everyone in such a holiday mood that the babble went on.

Finally, seizing the microphone, he SHOUTED into it the Lord's Prayer. The luncheon guests quickly quieted down.

Clarence Goshorn, who became president of the agency in 1942 soon after Pearl Harbor (with Hobler moving up to chairman), was a witty, cool, relaxed man, with a touch of the actor about him. (After a few drinks, he often recited Shakespeare—not single lines, but whole soliloquies.) Striding down Madison Avenue, bareheaded, wearing his familiar bow tie and smoking a pipe, he looked more like the college professor he had been than an advertising man. "Clancy," as he was called by his friends, enjoyed telling people he had been fired from an early job with the Curtis Publishing Company by the great *Saturday Evening Post* editor, George Horace Lorimer. This led him into advertising, first with Erwin, Wasey (where he worked with Hobler on Oxydol), then with Arthur Kudner. He joined B&B in 1937 and, after Lusk left, shared account management responsibility with Hobler. He is remembered by a former associate as "a superb salesman, a canny adviser for troubled situations and a wise and cautious copy editor."

"I never change copy," Goshorn once said, "unless I can persuade the writer that my suggestions are improvements." This was in the days when account men sometimes acted as their own creative directors, much to the exasperation of the actual CDs, although if an account person was ever qualified for the job, it was the erudite Goshorn.

Billings, after the departure of Colgate, had dropped to less than $10 million in 1942, and in the stress and dislocation of mobilizing for war, the nation's advertisers had little time to think about changing advertising agencies. No new accounts came into the shop in 1942.

A number of B&Bers enlisted or were drafted into the armed forces. One of them, Ted Steele, after marrying aspiring actress Marjorie Dalberg, joined the 20th Air Force, served in both the European and Pacific theaters, and was one of the producers of the *Army Hour*.

With the war drawing millions from the work force, industry was discovering a great untapped source of manpower—*womanpower*—and the advertising industry was turning to the same source. Advertising had for some time offered career opportunities for women at certain middle management levels in research, media, copy and publicity, but not, for some years to come, in account management. Now the number of women employees increased sharply. As Bill Tompkins, head of the art studio, recently recalled, "the bull pen during the war was mostly women—with a sprinkling of men with weak eyes."

A Wartime "Harem"

One man who gave full career opportunity to women was creative head Henry O. (Pat) Pattison, Jr. A tall, silver-haired engineering graduate of MIT, Pattison came to advertising by way of McGraw-Hill where he edited a technical magazine before joining J. Walter Thompson. (Pattison showed an early professional interest in women. The first ad he ever wrote, for *Redbook*, had the headline: "Behind Every Woman Stands a Man.") Among the writers on Pattison's wartime staff (he called it his "harem" in those pre-women's lib days) were Dorothy Whitney who always wore a hat in the office, Andy Talbert, Betty Pike and Helen Klintrup. All four eventually were made copy supervisors, and were among the first women in the advertising industry to become vice-presidents.

Pattison, a soft-spoken, pipe-smoking man with wary blue eyes, had a stormy beginning at B&B. Recently at his desert ranch outside Tucson, where he lives in retirement with his wife Mary, he recalled his early years with the agency.

· "I was hired in 1942 by Bill Day, the creative director, whom I'd worked under at Thompson. I was supposed to be copy chief. Only trouble was, they already had one, Jerry Carson, who regarded me as just another writer. I went in to see Hobe. 'Mr. Hobler,' I said, 'something's cockeyed.' When Hobe learned Day had hired me without consulting him, he flew into a rage, threw papers on the floor and ordered me to 'Get out!' Bill Day left after six months, and we ended up having *two* creative departments, Carson's and mine. It was typical of Hobe to keep things divided, play one against the other. I finally asked Hobe for a showdown, and Carson left. It was a tense, bitter time for three or four years."

Pattison's corner office on the eighth floor at 444 Madison was directly under Hobler's on the ninth floor. "Whenever Hobe wanted to see me," he recalls, "and that was three or four times a day, he used to stomp on the floor. I was at his beck and call, as everybody else was."

When Pattison arrived, Bill Benton still had an office at the agency, and Pattison described his first meeting with the former B&B partner.

"I went into his office and Benton was sitting at his desk with this vacuum massage apparatus on his head, like a space helmet. He was also dictating, having his nails manicured and his shoes shined. He invited me to lunch and when we got sat down, he said, 'Well! Tell me all about yourself.' I opened my mouth, but before I could say anything Benton started talking about *himself*, and never stopped talking all during lunch."

Both Pattison and Carson, uneasy as their alliance was, participated in new business solicitations. One presentation, prepared in 1943 for McKesson-Robbins, described the agency's "Creative Procedures":

> 1. Learn as much about the product, its ingredients, and its superiority as possible.
> 2. Try to develop a sound basic selling idea and "reason why" that grows out of *the product itself*.

The agency's founders: William Benton (above) and Chester Bowles. Benton left the agency in 1935 for a career in education, government and publishing. Bowles resigned in 1941 to become OPA administrator during W.W. II. Later, he was Governor of Connecticut, Undersecretary of State, and twice Ambassador to India.

The first campaign for the agency's first account, General Foods' Certo. Testimonial format was an innovation of Bowles, who was responsible for the agency's creative work during the beginning years.

Atherton W. Hobler, central figure in the life of the agency for more than a third of a century at about the time he became an equal partner with Benton and Bowles, in 1932. Hobler brought to the marriage a sizable dowry of about $5 million in General Foods billings.

Charles Winniger as Cap'n Andy on Showboat, *top-rated radio variety show of the mid-'30s, created by Bowles and sponsored by Maxwell House Coffee.*

Jack Haley, a regular on Showboat.

The Prudential Family Hour, *another popular radio show of the '30s and early '40s, sponsored by the insurance company. From left: Deems Taylor, Gladys Swarthout, orchestra leader Al Goodman. In the mid-'30s, the top three shows on the air were agency-produced, and B&B was known as the "hot young radio agency."*

The inimitable Fanny Brice as Baby Snooks starred, along with Frank Morgan, in Maxwell House Coffee Time, *which replaced* Showboat *in the early '40s.*

Young Dr. Malone, *an early daytime serial created by Chet Bowles which ran intermittently from the late '30s until 1961. Originally sponsored by General Foods, it was later bought by Procter & Gamble.*

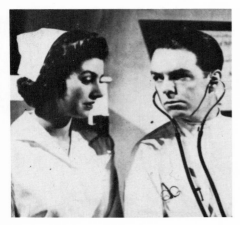

Everybody looks happy except the client! Maxwell House Coffee Advertising Manager Bob Bennett with George Burns (left), Gracie Allen, and Ted Steele, then head of the Hollywood office. The Burns and Allen Show was sponsored by Maxwell House during the late '40s.

Log Cabin Syrup was one of six General Foods products that Atherton Hobler brought from Erwin, Wasey to B&B in 1932.

Another innovation by Chet Bowles: the comic strip ad, forerunner of the TV slice-of-life format.

Huskies, Post cereal introduced in 1935, folded in 1942 despite a testimonial campaign featuring top athletes. Lou Gehrig, appearing in a radio commercial for the brand, made an historic boo-boo when he called Huskies "Wheaties."

Clarence Goshorn, Shakespeare-quoting ex-English professor, served as president from 1942 to 1950. He died in December 1950 when he fell from a dock in Bimini and drowned.

William R. Baker began as an assistant to Hobler in 1933 and became, successively, executive vice-president, president, chairman of the board, and honorary chairman. He retired in 1963, and died in 1975 at the age of 75.

Colgate, a major client until 1940, was also a heavy user of comic strip ads, many of them written by copy chief Walter O'Meara. The agency suffered one of its worst reverses when Colgate. . . .

. . . was spirited away by B&B account supervisor Ted Bates, who set up his own agency with Colgate and Continental Baking accounts totaling $4.5 million in billings.

Rosser Reeves, then a B&B copywriter, joined Bates at his new agency, where he rose to chairman of the board. He is author of Reality in Advertising, and now heads Rosser Reeves, Inc.

A.M. (Gil) Gilbert, partner of B&B's law firm, Davis & Gilbert, and legal counsel to the agency for 35 years. The only non-employee to be elected to the board of directors, he retired from that body in 1970 and was named director emeritus.

Bonnie Cox, secretary to Chester Bowles, and later the agency's first woman account executive, worked on the Walter Baker chocolate account.

Eddie Schneeberg, Chet Bowles' first office boy, joined the agency a month after it opened its doors; eventually he headed the radio copy department. The ad Schneeberg has on his desk is for Conn's Udder Ointment, possibly done for Hobler, who had a prize-winning herd of 200 Guernsey dairy cows.

Comic strip ads were also known as "doghouse strips," so-called because the archetypal strip had a picture of a man who'd been consigned by his wife to a real doghouse.

Account supervisor Frank Smith consulting his "little fact book" of marketing data which he carried, some said, next to his heart. For 27 years he guided the destiny of the agency's first assignment, Procter & Gamble's Ivory Snow—the longest service on a brand in P&G's and B&B's histories. He later became management supervisor and a director.

An early Ivory Snow ad when the product was sold for fine fabrics, before it was positioned as a product for baby wash.

Art shows have a long history at B&B. This one, in the late '40s, was attended by (from left) production manager Austin Thomas; creative director Pat Pattison; executive vice-president Bob Lusk; art director Joe Clark; chairman and chief executive officer Atherton Hobler; president Clarence Goshorn; executive vice-president Bill Baker; and art director Fred Truchess.

OPA administrator Bowles had plenty of critics in the business community—although he was a hero to President Truman and housewives at the checkout counter. After the war, when he became what was called "Economic Stabilizer," criticism mounted among advertisers. In a curious turn of events, the agency found itself writing ads like the one opposite for its client, the National Association of Manufacturers.

The picture that almost got Ted Steele lynched. To get a closeup shot for this Kentucky Pride ad, Steele, then account executive on Calvert, asked the photographer to get right out on the track. When the flashbulb went off, the leading horse shied and the others piled up. "We just made it out the gate ahead of the crowd," said Steele.

AT THE FAMOUS KENTUCKY DERBY...THEY'RE
PROUD OF **Kentucky Pride!**
A CALVERT WHISKEY

AROUND THE FIRST TURN they go-
breakneck speed. Nearly 100,0
spectators cheer themselves hoa
as the favorite begins to step out
front of the field. A fine day, a f
track, and an impressive list of ent
all helped to make the 1937 De
one of the most colorful in histo

"WHEN THE RACES ARE OVER,
I sure enjoy a nice drink of
Kentucky Pride," says Jockey
Hubert Callahan (left).

"IT WOULDN'T BE DERBY DAY without a drink of Kentucky
Pride," says Mr. Gilbert Glendening of Louisville (second
from right). "We Kentuckians are conservative drinkers,
but we do like to celebrate big occasions with a drink of
this fine Bourbon." Kentucky Pride is sold everywhere.

"I'M NOT MUCH ON PICKING THE HO
admits Mr. S. E. Duncan of Louisvill
being a Kentuckian—I can hold m
with anybody when it comes to pic
good whiskey. And in my opinio
Kentucky Pride is as fine a Bourbon
ever come across."

Calvert's **Kentucky Prid**

KENTUCKY STRAIGHT BOURBON...SMOOTH AND SATISFYING

YOU'LL
LIKE THE
PRICE,
TOO!

Calvert's
Kentucky Pride
KENTUCKY STRAIGHT
BOURBON WHISKEY

90 PROOF   Copr. 1937 CALVERT DISTILLERS CORP., DISTILLERIES: LOUISVILLE, KY., AND RELAY, MD., EXECUTIVE OFFICES: CHRYSLER BLDG., N. Y. C.

3. Dramatize the idea in space or on the air in a
manner that is distinctive from competitive advertising,
and creates the right quality or impression about the product.

In the same McKesson-Robbins presentation, the agency
threw modesty to the winds and did a little bragging about its 18-
member research staff, headed by William R. Farrell as director, and
William Keenan as manager: "Without hesitation, we can say that
ours is one of the two or three finest research departments in the
advertising business."

To back up its boast, no fewer than thirteen research activities
were listed including marketing research, product research, sales testing, premium testing, copy testing and evaluation of Starch, Hooper,
Clark and Crossley reports.

The presentation was a success and it landed the McKesson-
Robbins account, just one of eleven new clients added during the
three-year period 1942–45, boosting billings to $15 million in 1944,
the first time that level was regained in five years. The new accounts
included American Magazine, Can Manufacturers Institute, Florida
Citrus (which former BBDO president Charlie Brower once called
"the wandering comet of the advertising skies"), Bituminous Coal
Institute, Pepperell and the Association of American Railroads.

The agency almost didn't get the Railroad account. During the
presentation, a crusty railroad president asked why in hell the Association should hire an agency named after those two damned liberal
Democrats, Benton and Bowles? Clarence Goshorn, after explaining
that neither of the original partners now had any connection with the
agency, went on to say: "To use a railroad analogy, sir: the Atchison,
Topeka & Santa Fe is a great railroad. It is great despite the fact that
it does not start in Atchison, does not go through Topeka, and does
not terminate in Santa Fe."

The president saw the point and withdrew his objection.

Get Rid of "Benton & Bowles"?

After both Bowles and Benton became prominent in the Democratic administration (Bowles as Administrator of the Office of Price Administration, Benton as Assistant Secretary of State under Jimmy Byrnes), there was serious discussion among the top executives about changing the agency's name. Hobler's original contract with the corporation gave him the right to add his name to the firm's name. But now the mood of some was to eliminate the founders' names altogether. John Cobb, account supervisor for the Association of American Railroads, strongly favored getting rid of the "Benton & Bowles" name. A major client representative—a Republican, as most clients were—was unhappy with Bowles's price control policies and urged a change. At the annual stockholders' meeting in 1946, Hobler announced his decision: "Bob Lusk said to me, 'The idea of disowning two bright young men who had worked hard to create the business is distasteful to me.' I agree with Bob. J. Walter Thompson and Young & Rubicam didn't change their names when the original principals left. I think the name should remain Benton & Bowles."

The reason Hobler rejected the idea of adding his name, according to Gilbert, was his feeling that "Hobler sounds too Teutonic," that it "doesn't seem to go with Benton & Bowles."

The firm name remained unchanged. There is little doubt that its retention was a liability in some of the agency's attempts to get new business. For many years, almost the first question prospects would ask, according to a former executive, was "Are Benton and Bowles still associated with the agency?" The persistence of this public impression was to prove a liability to both Benton and Bowles as well during their public careers. Benton's biographer, Sidney Hyman, writes, " . . . no matter what he did or how he did it, he always had to buck the suspicion that he was just another Madison Avenue phrasemonger."

Benton, on a radio interview program in 1970, said, "Hardly a week goes by that somebody still doesn't ask if I am still connected with Benton & Bowles."

"Paging Mr. Bowles"

Advertisers, and the National Association of Manufacturers,

had little love for OPA Administrator Bowles, and even less for Economic Stabilizer Bowles, the title he assumed in the postwar price-control body. In a curious turn of events, B&B got the NAM account the same year Bowles was named Economic Stabilizer, and found itself in an awkward situation. Bowles describes it in his autobiography: "I was particularly disturbed to read full-page advertisements demanding that I change our OPA policies prepared by my old firm, Benton & Bowles. . . ." The ads, headlined "Paging Mr. Bowles," urged Bowles "to remove price controls on manufactured goods, and production will step up fast."

Wartime Radio

Radio programming during the war years reflected the national state of mind—its intense concern over the Battle of Britain, the air raids against Hitler on the Continent, the war in the Pacific. News became the Number One staple. Post Toasties sponsored Boake Carter, and later Elmer Davis, whose Indiana twang had a down-home reassurance that made him, next to H. V. Kaltenborn, the most popular news commentator on the air, so popular President Roosevelt called Davis to Washington to head the Office of War Information. Soap operas, too, reflected the realities of war: P&G's *Ma Perkins*, the folksy philosopher of Rushville Center, lost her son John in the war, and he was "buried somewhere in Europe in an unmarked grave." The agency's *Prudential Hour*, starring Gladys Swarthout, Deems Taylor, and Al Goodman's Orchestra, featured dramatic tributes to, as the program's script reads, "the indomitable nations united with us in the worldwide fight for freedom."

The director of the *Prudential Hour* was Tom McDermott, known at the time as "the Boy Wonder of B&B." (At 22 he became the agency's youngest vice-president.) McDermott, whose father was a bellhop in the old Belmont Hotel, grew up on the lower East Side, worked his way through Manhattan College and Columbia manning the theater ticket counter in the Gotham Hotel. He started at B&B, as almost everybody did, in the mailroom, but had already gotten his feet wet in radio, writing freelance scripts for Elaine Carrington's *When a Girl Marries* at $20 a script. One of McDermott's problems was his youthful, wet-behind-the-ears appearance—he was always being mistaken for a messenger boy. But there was nothing wet behind the ears about his canny knowledge of the medium. When Walter Craig became head of radio, replacing Kirby Hawkes, McDermott became his assistant, and eventually headed the department. He had a special father-son relationship with Hobler, who continued to have an active interest in radio, and later, TV production.

"If he got sick, watch out," McDermott recalled recently in California, where he lives with his actress wife, Ann Burr, and their two children, and heads his own production company. "He'd stay home and watch all the daytime shows, then come in with a detailed critique of the plots, the actors, even the music bridges. Ever since *Showboat* days he regarded himself as a production expert. He had a temper, as we all know. One time, we had a big argument in his office about a show. Hobe was making an emphatic point, and he slams his hand down on the desk so hard he smashes his watch. He looks at it, aghast, and cries, 'Now look what you made me do—break my good watch!' But he always backed up his people. Walter Craig had this show, *Those Two*, starring Pinky Lee and Vivian Blaine—a real dog— he was trying to sell to P&G. Gail Smith (P&G Productions) hated it, and Walter was getting nowhere until Hobe walked into the meeting. Gail asks Hobe, 'Do you support the agency's recommendation?' Hobe said he did. So P&G finally bought the show. Funny thing was, Hobe didn't especially like the show. But he backed up Walter and the agency's right to recommend programming."

"What are you doing . . . television-wise?"

As early as 1943, in the midst of the war, Procter & Gamble was thinking about television. In a letter to Hobler, Bill Ramsey of P&G Productions, wrote, "Will you please tell us what you are doing today television-wise for your other clients?"

Ramsey, a dapper, fastidious man who wore gray flannel

chalk-striped suits, always with a red carnation in the lapel (and, it is said, had his secretary wash his money every morning), asked Compton, another P&G agency, the same question. There is nothing in the record to indicate what, if anything, B&B did in response to Ramsey's letter, but Wyllis Cooper, a Compton producer, eventually wrote a comprehensive, witty report on the state of the art in 1944–45.

A chief worry of just about everybody who had anything to do with television was what they considered the outlandish costs of programming, compared to radio. Cooper, while on the West Coast, had investigated a number of cost-cutting production techniques and possible sources of programs presented to him by a motley crew of "producers." His report, in part, follows:

> In Hollywood I was approached by literally scores of *soi-disant* producers of films-for-televison . . . legions of earnest ex-corporals breathed down my neck as they supplied the dialogue and Disneyesque sound effects for their confections. I saw more bowling balls turn into cigarette packages, more terra-cotta animated figures pretending to sing "Old Black Joe". . . . One highly touted "commerical" producer showed me the birth of our Saviour in underexposed Kodachrome, which consisted of six reels of extras in colored nightgowns leading assorted livestock up and down the hills of Iverson's ranch. . . . I was harangued by a man whose idea of cutting costs on television production is to build half-size sets and use midget actors. . . .

The conclusion of Cooper's report was that, yes, television was going to cost a bundle, and that ultimately most programming would be on film—a prediction that eventually proved to be accurate after an initial period of live broadcasting, and before videotape.

"Plant Victory in Your Back Yard"

The war saw advertising assume a new role in the communications world. The industry whose skills of persuasion had helped move billions of dollars' worth of goods and services for its clients now put those skills to use in the public interest. The War Advertising Council was formed two months after Pearl Harbor, and Benton

& Bowles, along with some 25 other advertising agencies, advertisers and media members took on the job of informing the public about such matters as war bonds, recruitment of nurses, morale, civil defense and conservation of scarce materials. The agency's first public service campaign urged people to plant victory gardens. This was followed by Food Fights for Freedom, and campaigns for basic nutrition and conservation of tin.

Thus began the agency's long and continuing involvement in public service campaigns. After V-E Day, with "War" dropped from its title, the Advertising Council expanded its activities into many new areas of public concern. Its campaign for traffic safety is credited with saving more than 600,000 lives in twenty years. A memorable ten-year Better Schools campaign, prepared by B&B, was cited by the Council as being responsible for boosting PTA membership more than 100 percent, and increasing contributions to colleges 329 percent. Through the years other B&B public service efforts have included campaigns for the USO ("Winning the Peace is a lonely Battle"); UNICEF ("Some of the Saddest Children in the World are Starting to Smile"); the American Cancer Society, which had a campaign urging women to examine their own breasts ("Cancer. Sometimes You Can Put Your Finger On It"); and since 1971, the Muscular Dystrophy Association. The annual Jerry Lewis Labor Day Telethon for MDA has raised a total of more than $170 million in the last eight years.

Not all the agency public service campaigns have been successful. One, an in-house campaign publicizing the contributions of the Advertising Council itself, backfired. The campaign featured a message printed on blank B&B salary checks, enclosed in the regular salary check envelope. When they were distributed a day before payday, a lot of people thought, "Wow! Pay day's a day early!" and rushed down to the bank in the building without opening the envelopes. When they did, standing in the tellers' lines, and read "No, this isn't your check, it represents the contribution the Advertising Council makes, etc.," there were some pretty nasty things said about the two people who dreamed up the idea, copywriters Brian Dillon and Sid Lerner.

"A Statesman of His Profession"

The man most closely associated with the public service activities at Benton & Bowles from the war years until his retirement in 1963, was William Reginald Baker, Jr., who joined the agency in 1933 as Atherton Hobler's assistant. A six-foot-two Princeton graduate (in the '30s he looked like a tall Ivy League version of Rudolph Valentino), he used to weekend occasionally in New York where he fell in love with the star of a George M. Cohan musical comedy. "When I was with her," Baker said, "she made the bathtub gin taste like champagne." After college, he worked as a clerk in one of the grocery stores of a chain founded by his grandfather. In a sense, he never left the grocery business; for most of his forty years at B&B, except for two years as manager of the Hollywood office, he supervised the General Foods account. Along the way he became, successively, executive vice-president, president, chairman of the board and, in 1963, honorary chairman. His volunteer work began with the War Advertising Council, and continued until 1963 when he was named chairman of that organization.

"Bill was a gentleman and a gentle man," a longtime associate said recently. "Bob Lusk once asked Bill to go out to California to fire a senior production supervisor who'd been with the company for many years. Bill went out, spent a couple of days with the guy, had drinks and dinner with him, but just couldn't bring himself to fire him. Bill came back to New York and the man stayed on for another ten years until he retired."*

Baker died March 11, 1975, at the age of 76.

Taking a cue from Bill Baker, many individual B&Bers have contributed their time and talent to public service. For three years in the late '50s, a group of stage-struck employees formed the Off-Madison Avenue Players and put on three productions for the benefit of The Lighthouse and a child shelter in Brooklyn. The lead of one,

---

*At BBDO some years ago, an art director was called in and told he was fired. "*Fired?!*" the man cried. "Do you realize how busy I am? I can't possibly leave," and he reeled off all the things he was working on. "Don't bother me with that nonsense, I haven't got time," he said, and stalked out. He was still there 25 years later.

Say, Darling, was Nancy Ford, coproducer in 1978 of the musical hit *I'm Getting My Act Together and Taking It On the Road*. When *As the World Turns* executive producer Fred Bartholomew, a former child actor, was asked to accept a part in *Say, Darling*, he refused, having emphatically sworn off acting after a somewhat unhappy and exploited Hollywood childhood. "And if you mention it again," Bartholomew said at the time, "I'll cut you dead at the elevators!"

One recently retired B&Ber, Andy Fescina, quietly did good work in the anonymity of the photostat and mailrooms which he supervised for many years, while also running the agency's security operation. A self-taught electronics technician, Fescina repaired more than a thousand radios, TV sets, electric trains and hearing aids for New York Community Services. Fescina also performed another little-known social service: In a program initiated in 1967 by former creative director Whit Hobbs, a total of more than 200 emotionally handicapped people, referred to the agency by Fountain House, were under Fescina's supervision, working as messengers and duplicating operators.*

A slim, muscular physical-fitness devotee who works out daily in a gym, Fescina is a man with many irons in the fire. He began at B&B as assistant to Lenny Levin, then head of the photostat room, where one of his sidelines was giving haircuts during lunch hour. "I learned how to barber from a seven-page pamphlet," Fescina recalls, "but somebody tore out the page that told how to finish up. So I was never able to really finish a haircut."

Levin, a round beach-ball of a man from Brooklyn, always with a ready quip, had a few sidelines himself. In addition to showing stag films (that was before the word "porno" was invented) in his darkroom at 25¢ a standee (there were no chairs), he played vibes in a B&B jazz group,** and ran a horse parlor. Bill Tompkins remembers the betting operation:

"We'd place our bets with Lenny and he'd write out the slips.

---

*As a result of this work, Fescina was invited by President Nixon in 1971 to speak before the President's Conference on the Employment of the Handicapped. For two hours, five hundred psychologists, psychiatrists and mental health counselors listened enthralled to Fescina's non-professional but practical advice.

**The other members: Fescina and TV art director Ray Lind, trumpets; music director Len McKenzie, piano; Ted Steele, drums; and a window washer—name unknown—on washtub bass.

One day a cop friend of mine comes up to see me in his uniform, and somebody misdirects him to the photostat room. When he walks in, Lenny thinks it's a raid, and washes all the day's slips down the sink. I was mad, because I had a winner that day."

The betting operation was finally Levin's undoing. In debt to outside bookies, he let them use the agency's night line, and this time the police did raid the place. A detective called on Hobler the next day —and Levin, after fifteen years at B&B, was out on the street.

"When I heard Lenny was fired, I knew the days of the sidelines was over," said Fescina. "I stopped right in the middle of cutting George McAndrew's (an art director) hair—and I never cut another head of hair again."

Devoted to the ponies to the end, Levin worked until his death in 1978 as a publicity man for the New York State Harness Racing Association.

"The most competitive man I ever knew "

Hobler didn't enjoy firing Lenny Levin. He didn't like to fire anyone, and usually left the job to somebody else. Despite his fierce exterior—his eyes could arrest, try and find a man guilty with one piercing look—he had a forgiving heart, although he did a pretty good job of hiding it under a tough competitiveness.

"Hobe will fight anybody in the alley for twenty-five bucks," Bob Lusk once said.

"He was the most competitive man I ever knew," said a former associate. "He wanted to win at everything—backgammon, gin rummy, golf, soft ball, Ping-Pong, bridge." Austin Johnson, retired former director of promotion, recently told about playing gin rummy with Hobler. "I used to fly to Florida with Hobe in the company plane to see the Florida Citrus people, and we'd play gin all the way down. If he was behind when we landed, we'd sit in the plane an hour, two hours, as long as it took for him to get ahead."

His determination to dominate extended even to elevators. "When we moved to 666 [Fifth Avenue] where they had automatic elevators," Johnson recalls, "Hobe tried to do the same thing he did in the old building, command the operator to take him nonstop to his floor. The first day in the new building he got in an UP elevator on his floor and said to the near-empty car, 'Down.' When it went up instead, he shouted, 'Dammit, I said DOWN!' "

His chief interest in life, next to his business and his family (his wife Ruth Wells Hobler and four children), was his prize-winning 200-head herd of Guernsey dairy cows.

"Sometimes I thought the cows came before the family," said Mert Sowerby, manager for 25 years of the Hobler 260-acre farm, Woodacres, outside Princeton, New Jersey. "Every night when he came home," Sowerby said, "he'd start blowing his horn 600 feet from the barn, so somebody would be out there to greet him. He always went to the barn first to see his cows." And being a winner, his cows had to be winners, too, which they were. Between 1955 and 1970, Woodacres had more grand champions than any other farm in the country. (At an American Guernsey Club convention in Phoenix in 1963, Hobler ran for director and lost. Piqued, he packed up and left. If he couldn't win, he didn't want to play.)

He had little patience with things he couldn't control. He wanted to take time itself and bend it to his will. Ray Lind, TV art director and later a producer, describes Hobler reading a one-minute TV commercial: "It was just too long—kept coming out at 1:13, and Hobe kept reading it faster and faster, trying by sheer will to get it down to a minute." Time was always his enemy. Every dash to the Princeton station was a photo finish, every trip to the railroad station or airport a race against the clock.

Frank Smith remembers a memorable sprint for a train. "Hobe was on his way to Cincinnati for an Ivory Snow meeting, and I helped him down to the street with his charts and portfolio and tried to find a cab. When none appeared, Hobe stepped out into the street, commandeered a panel truck, and talked the driver into taking him to Penn Station."

Time was a protagonist he would have strangled with his bare hands, if he could have. On his fiftieth birthday, an old friend recalls, he "had the feeling that his life was over. His father had died young and he thought he would, too." He was, in fact, plagued by ill health the last thirty years of his life; he had diabetes, gout and a circulatory ailment in his legs.

Hobler's youngest son, Herbert Wells Hobler, now 55 and owner of the Nassau Broadcasting Company in Princeton, remembers his father as a strict but fair disciplinarian, a man driven by a will to dominate every situation. Of the four children (the others: Ed, Wells and Virginia who died at 27), Herb was the only one who stood up to him.

"I was the rebel," Herb said recently. "One time I told him, 'You're so goddamn *right* all the time!' We had plenty of fights, and more than once he got out his leather belt. But in later years he mellowed. When I was about forty, I remember he said to me, 'I'm glad you fought me. I wish your brothers had done the same.' " Ed and Wells both worked for several years as account executives at Benton & Bowles—the only exceptions to the agency's rule against nepotism—before taking up other business careers.

He liked people who gave him a little resistance—up to a point. Art director Dick Ende recalls a meeting he and copywriter Ed Bihl had with Hobler on some Lady Schick copy.

"Hobe was sitting behind his desk and Ed was presenting the ads. Hobe kept rejecting them, rejecting them, until Bihl, discouraged, threw in the towel. Then Hobe banged on the desk and said, 'Dammit, Ed! You caved in too fast! Let me show you how to do it.' And he took our place on the other side of the desk and presented the ads to *us.*"

"Call Gil"

A. M. Gilbert's first encounter with Hobler was in 1935 when he became the agency's counsel.

"Watch out for Black Mike,"* Tom Revere warned Gilbert who had been hired by Bowles. "My first assignment from Hobe was to arrange a charter party. I didn't know from nothing about charter

---

*A nickname given Hobler (he had a black mustache) by Charles Winninger, who played Cap'n Andy on *Showboat*

parties, but I figured it had something to do with boats, so I go to the library and read up on maritime law—became an expert on it! Turned out, all he wanted was to lease a boat to take some clients out on the river."

Talking about his long association with the agency that began with the three partners, Gilbert observed, "Bowles said I talked too fast, Hobe said I talked too slow, and Benton said I talked too much."

Probably no man was closer to Hobler during his long agency career than Albert Milton Gilbert, former summer camp rabbi and honor graduate of Columbia Law School, whose father started as a peddler with a horse and wagon in Fall River, Massachusetts. The only nonemployee ever elected a director of Benton & Bowles, he was a familiar figure at stockholders' meetings, sitting close to Hobler, leaning over from time to time to whisper advice. A quick-moving man of medium build, with a razor-keen mind, a wizened right arm, swarthy complexion and deep-set dark eyes, he was the first man the agency turned to when a legal problem arose—or any other problem, for that matter. The automatic response to crises, business or personal, large or small, was "Call Gil." He settled law suits, lobbied (successfully) to repeal restrictive dairy laws aimed against Best Foods' Nucoa; kept the minutes of board meetings (the early ones were held informally in Hobler's office); wrote contracts (sometimes dictating them to an agency secretary while he stood by her desk); devised sophisticated stock purchase plans for employees; wrote deferred-compensation agreements (the first in the industry); arranged divorces; wrote wills; handled details of sudden and tragic deaths; and was always there, night or day, when he was needed.

"One time," he recalls, "my daughter got sick—a stomach ache. I called the doctor, then right after that Hobe called me to come over. I did, and my daughter had her appendix out while I wasn't there. I hope she forgave me. B&B has been my family as much as my own."

Gilbert, who retired with Hobler from the board in 1970, remembers him as a man of unusual integrity. "He had his faults," he said, "but I never knew him to do or say anything he should be ashamed of. He was very, very honest. One time we were in Washington walking past the old Willard Hotel, and Hobe had to make a phone call. He goes into a pay booth and pretty soon comes out with his hands full of coins. 'What do I do with this?' he asks me. 'I guess you hit the jackpot,' I says. 'No,' he says, 'I've got to get it back to them.' So, standing on the street, we count the money, and when he gets home, he sends a check for the amount to the telephone company." He laughed, remembering. "He always took me to the men's room with him, so he could keep on talking. More damned decisions were made there. The decision to make Bob Lusk president was made in the men's room!"

Although Hobler could be frugal—he gave Herb 20c a week allowance when he was growing up in Bronxville—he was generous in other ways. He helped several young people through college, including most of his sixteen grandchildren. He also paid the medical school expenses of a young family friend, David Speer.

"I called him Picklepuss," Dr. Speer recalled recently. "Why, I don't remember. We had a kidding kind of man-to-man relationship, even though I was about the age of his son Eddie." Speer, 61, a lean, hard-as-nails general surgeon with a crew haircut, said he used to go deep-sea fishing with Hobler. "He loved to fight a big fish. He was a powerful man. Could do one-arm pushups well into his sixties. One time he lost his new Abercrombie & Fitch watch over the side. 'STOP THE BOAT!' he shouts." Speer laughed. "So typical of him. Somebody, by God, was going right down to the bottom of the ocean and retrieve that watch! I remember when the agency lost Colgate. End of the world! Gloom and doom! But you know what pulled him out of it? That same week Dick Francis, Clarence Francis's son, was killed in an auto accident just before his wedding. Hobe says to me, 'Here I am moaning about a lost account, and there's poor Clare who's lost a son.' It restored his perspective and he snapped out of it."

The loss of Colgate by now was but a memory, like an old war wound that ached only on rainy days. The association with Procter & Gamble steadily prospered, and in the fall of 1945 the agency received the promised assignment of Product X, the product Howard Morgens had said might "revolutionize the entire soap industry."

Billings for 1945 rose to $15 million and in a tradition begun with the first offering of stock to employees in 1935, the agency shared its bounty by inaugurating a profit sharing plan in 1944, another industry first originated by Gilbert. The first year 155 members of the B&B family participated, and the company paid 12.47 percent of eligible employees' salaries into the fund. By 1978 the fund had grown to more than $18 million, and disbursements from it to employees during the 34 years of its existence amounted to about $23 million.

A Prodigal Son Returns

Early in 1944 Bob Lusk, who had left the agency in 1941, came to see Hobler. After a brief stint at Bates in charge of the Colgate account, Ed Little had persuaded Lusk to join him at Colgate as executive vice-president, replacing former B&B colleague Jim Adams, who had become president of Standard Brands. From Colgate, Lusk had gone to Pedlar & Ryan as a full partner, an association that soured when a number of top P&R people pulled out to form Dougherty, Shenfield & Steers (later Needham, Harper & Steers). Now, tired of playing musical chairs, Lusk told Hobler he "wanted to come home."*

Hobler was agreeable to his return, but Goshorn resented the idea, feeling that Lusk had been "disloyal" when he joined the Bates/Colgate exodus. But eventually, he and Bill Baker, by then executive vice-president, acceded to Hobler's wishes, and Lusk rejoined, with the understanding that he would have to start at the bottom. Within a year he was elected a vice-president and a member of the board. Shortly after, he was assigned account responsibility for Product X, which the washday world would soon know as Tide.

---

*People wanting to "come home" to B&B is a recurring phenomenon in the agency's history. Returning prodigal sons (and one daughter) include, in addition to Lusk, Herb Arnold, Ted Burnett, Ed Caffrey, Owen Evans, Jim Haines, Mildred Peterson, Shelly Platt, George Robinson, Jim Rogers, Earl Rowan, Ed Schneeberg, Jack Taylor, Gordon Vanderwalker.

The end of the war unleashed the energies, hopes and expectations of a nation weary of shortages and hungering for consumer goods. Like a family that had kept a light burning in the window, Benton & Bowles awaited the return of its veteran sons, and began to prepare for the most dramatic burst of activity and growth in the agency's history.

Five

The Detergent Decade
1946–55

$\mathcal{V}$E Day . . . VJ Day . . . The wonderful postwar world. . . .

And it *was* wonderful for the millions lucky enough to come home. To the returning veterans, and the families and friends that welcomed them, Norman Corwin's *On A Note of Triumph*, broadcast on CBS as hostilities ended in Europe, had a special poignance:

> . . . Lord God of fresh bread and tranquil mornings . . .
> Deliver notice to the fallen young men
> That tokens of orange juice and whole egg
> Appear now before the hungry children;
> That night again falls cooling on the earth
> As quietly as when it leaves your hand. . . .

With the surrender of the Japanese, the communications and advertising industries lost little time in getting back to business-as-usual (except that 'usual' would never be usual again—if it ever was). Within days after VJ Day President Truman approved the manufacture of radio receivers and television sets. Agencies and the networks offered their returning heroes their old jobs back or comparable ones, and NBC invited ex-GI actors to drop in for "welcome home" auditions.

At Benton & Bowles, to deal with what it termed "the reentry problem," management readied a retraining program which *Printers Ink* called "B&B's College of Advertising Knowledge" (after Kay Kyser's *Kollege of Musical Knowledge*, a popular radio show of the '40s). Developed by Brown Bolte' and administered by Quentin

McDonald, the program had some ninety enrollees and ran for 76 weeks. Courses consisted of instruction in all phases of agency activity, and featured guest speakers such as Ralph Starr Butler and Charles Mortimer of General Foods, and Howard Morgens of Procter & Gamble.

Among the returning vets was Ted Steele who, having had a taste of show business as a producer of the *Army Hour*, decided he wanted to transfer from account management to the radio department. When he talked to General Manager Jim Adams about it, Adams's sardonic comment was, "What a quaint idea." Given a choice of working with Bob Lusk on Project X or becoming business manager of the radio department, Steele opted for the latter. The Project X assignment went to Alan Sidnam, a young Kalamazoo College graduate and ex-Air Force fighter pilot, just back from the Southwest Pacific with a hundred missions behind him and a hatful of medals, including the Purple Heart. Another Air Force veteran was John Masson, who was hired to pilot the new company plane, a Beechcraft Bonanza, quickly christened by the troops "The Brasshopper."*

"Tide's In . . . Dirt's Out!"

When Procter & Gamble, after 200,000 man-hours of experimentation, finally developed a synthetic detergent for heavy-duty laundry, some executives of the company were in favor of forgetting all about it.

They feared that such a product, according to Alfred Lief, author of *It Floats*, "might take away as much as half of the laundry soap sales. New machinery costs would run into hundreds of millions of dollars, while existing soap-making machinery would lie idle."

---

*The agency owned and operated propeller planes for fourteen years, until the jet age made them obsolete. One pilot, Sam Graves, was killed when his plane stalled out over Teterboro airport during takeoff. John Masson became an account executive on Texaco, and heads the agency's Texaco office in Houston.

But Neil McElroy, then assistant to president Richard R. Deupree, wanted to go ahead. "If we don't," he said, "somebody else will."

The idea of a synthetic detergent was not new. P&G had introduced Dreft, a light-duty soapless product and the first of its kind, in 1933, and Drene, a detergent shampoo in 1934. But Tide was the first product built for heavy-duty cleaning.

Originally, P&G thought it would supplement, but not supplant, soap products, and would have its biggest appeal in hard-water areas. At the company's annual stockholders' meeting in 1947, Deupree said: ". . . in my judgment there is small chance of synthetic detergents replacing soap products to any marked degree."

In a meeting at the agency, Neil McElroy told Atherton Hobler that the new product "might reach a 10 percent market share." P&G came to the agency with what it felt was the perfect claim: "Tide gets clothes cleaner than any soap." Research revealed, however, that the claim was not particularly impressive, that it sounded to consumers like the same kind of puffery they'd heard before from advertisers.

So the agency put its creative heads together and came up with a statement to precede the claim: "Out of the Procter & Gamble laboratories comes an amazing washday miracle." This rang bells with housewives, and indicated a confidence in the company and its products (and, it might be observed, a weakness for strong adjectives). The idea that powered the introductory campaign and helped drive the brand's message deep into the consciousness of postwar consumers was expressed in four little words. Alan Sidnam tells how the idea was born:

"I was in a meeting with Edward L. Bernays, the PR man P&G had hired to publicize Tide. Bernays was an eccentric, flamboyant man, much addicted to wild, extravagant ideas. He sat there musing out loud . . . 'Tide . . . the tide rolling in . . . the Bay of Fundy. . . . That's it! We'll have a box of Tide being washed ashore at the Bay of Fundy!' We didn't do anything with the Bay of Fundy, but that weekend I thought of the phrase, 'When the Tide comes in, the dirt goes out.' Monday morning I gave the line to Dorothy Whitney and, advertising pro that she was, she shortened it to 'Tide's In . . . Dirt's Out,' which was incorporated into a print ad and a jingle."

The 10-second jingle, written by Andy Love.* became the keystone of the introductory campaign. Using spot radio and an average of ten daytime and five nighttime shows a week, plus newspapers, the new product was launched, district by district, over a three-year period.

In every market opened, the story was the same: skyrocketing sales—two or three times more than the brand's objective, in soft-water as well as hard-water territories.

Production facilities were expanded, but P&G was hard-pressed to keep pace with the demand. By 1949 when Tide reached national distribution, it was outselling every laundry soap product in the country, including Lever Brothers' Rinso and P&G's own Oxydol.

And, as often happens with a successful brand, Tide's rising fortunes carried on its crest the careers of agency people closely associated with it, notably Bob Lusk and Alan Sidnam, both destined to rise in the agency's hierarchy.**

With a success like Tide on its hands, it wasn't long before every soap company in the country was taking pot shots at P&G. Colgate brought out Fab, Lever Brothers had Surf. But Tide had stolen a march on the whole gang. Tide's success was a clear signal to the Cincinnati soap maker that detergents were the wave of the future. (The market share of soap products dropped from 83 percent in 1946 to 7 percent in 1961.) During the next ten years or so—the detergent decade, as the industry called it—P&G launched nine synthetic de-

---

*The full jingle:

SINGERS:	Tide's in. . . . Dirt's out! T-I-D-E Tide!
ANNCR:	Tide gets clothes cleaner than any soap!
VOICE:	Any soap?
ANNCR:	Yes, *any* soap!
SINGERS:	Tide gets clothes cleaner than any soap. T-I-D-E Tide!

**Sidnam, recently recalling his early years on Tide, said one of his most vivid memories was of playing gin rummy with Hobler on the overnight Cincinnati Limited. "Bob Lusk and I went out to see Procter at least once a week," he said, "and Hobe often went along. Bob wouldn't play with him, so I was drafted—and I always lost. Finally I told him, 'Hobe, I only make $5,500 a year. I can't afford to lose all this money.' The following Monday, Hobe walked into my office and said, 'All right, Sidnam, I'm giving you a $500 raise, so you can play gin with me on the Cincinnati trips.' "

tergent products,* and invested more money in plant and equipment than it had during its first one hundred years.

.Looking back on the greatest growth period in the company's history, Richard Deupree, who moved to chairman in 1948, with McElroy as president, said: " . . . we did the job within our own pattern . . . within the lines we knew. . . . You do something you think is right. If it clicks, you give it a ride. If you hit, mortgage the farm and go to it. But you can't always hit, and when you don't, have sense enough to get out."**

Late in 1946 a Procter & Gamble brand group came to New York to brief the agency on another new product assignment, a concentrated shampoo, thicker than cream shampoos, that came in a collapsible metal tube—Prell Concentrate Shampoo. In his autobiography, Hobler describes the agency's reaction:

> "We appreciate your giving Benton & Bowles this business," I said at the end of the meeting. "We would have been disappointed if you had not." A quizzical look preceded the brand manager's question. "And why is that exactly?" Several years earlier, I explained, Bob Tannehill, a Benton & Bowles account executive, set forth in a memorandum to me . . . reasons for developing a collapsible tube shampoo . . . (which I sent to) P&G's drug division. There was much excitement at the time and . . . assurance that P&G would adopt the agency's suggestion.

Somewhere along the line it was forgotten that the idea had originated with B&B.

But this lapse of memory by its esteemed client didn't dampen the agency's satisfaction in seeing the new shampoo become "an instant and phenomenal success." In his autobiography, Hobler uses Prell Concentrate to make a point about marketing and the role an agency can play in developing new marketing opportunities for its clients:

---

*Tide (1946); Prell Shampoo (1947); Joy (1949); Cheer (1952); Dash (1954); Cascade (1955); Comet (1957); Zest (1958); Ivory Liquid (1958).

**Among the P&G products assigned to B&B over the years that did not "hit": Whirl (liquid shortening); Stardust (dry bleach); Pin-It (home permanent); and Winterset-Summerset (hair spray).

Prell became a success in the marketplace because the
product filled a need . . . brought new value to the consumer . . . the story of its success emphasizes the point
that creativity in advertising need not be measured alone
by copy and art or the broadcast commercial . . . with Prell
there was great creativity in "inventing" a new product.

"Amazing Coffee Discovery"

To any W.W. II veteran who remembers the vile dark liquid,
made from a C-ration packet of powder, that masqueraded as coffee,
it isn't hard to understand why soluble coffees were not exactly the
hottest items in the postwar market. Like Spam and Dear John letters,
soluble coffee had the taste of a time a lot of people wanted to forget.

General Foods had made its first shipments of Instant Maxwell House Coffee during the war from its new plant in Hoboken.
Three years later, with the product "aromatized," it was made available to the public. But nobody was much interested. The best the
brand could do was gain about a 5 percent share of the instant market.

The problem: The flavor didn't measure up to that of Nescafe
and Instant Sanka, the major competitors. It took General Foods two
years, but after developing and blind-testing some forty for-
mulations, it finally had a product that won hands down over all
other instants.

With a clearly superior product—the first prerequisite of
Hobler's "Triangle of Marketing Success"—the creative department
went to work on the second: memorable, persuasive copy. Creative
supervisor Dick Wylly was given the assignment, and within a week
had hammered together an introductory print ad that ran virtually
unchanged for the next seven years. The headline read: AMAZING COF-
FEE DISCOVERY. The copy, as neatly carpentered as a Chinese box, read:

Not a powder, not a grind, but millions of tiny flavor buds
of real coffee, ready to burst instantly into that famous
Good-to-the-Last-Drop flavor.

Wylly, a meticulous craftsman with a mordant wit (to him
there were two classes of people: "kiddies" and "groanies"), guarded

that classic hunk of copy with his life. If someone came into his office suggesting he change a word, or even a comma, he would scream, "Out! Out! It's working, leave it alone!"

And work it did. The same ad with the jar wreathed in an unearthly light, as if it had just descended from heaven, ran year after year in newspapers and *Life*. Tom Dunphy, an early TV copywriter, developed a distinctive demonstration in which announcer Rex Marshall showed the texture of the flavor buds under a magnifying glass, and made a cup of coffee right on camera. In one truly distinctive demonstration on live TV, Marshall added the hot water, and exactly on cue, as he said "burst instantly," the glass coffee cup shattered into a hundred pieces.

By emphasizing the flavor and good taste of the product, rather than the traditionally advertised advantages of convenience and economy, Instant Maxwell House became a runaway best-seller, eventually capturing a 40 percent share of the instant market.*

The Age of Television

> *"Television will either prove to be a saving radiance in the sky—or an unbearable disturbance of the peace."*
> —E.B. White

> *"They call television a medium because nothing on it is ever well done."*
> —Fred Allen

Television had its first faltering beginnings at Benton & Bowles in 1947 when two WOR radio shows, *Juvenile Jury* and *Meet the Press*, sponsored by General Foods, were converted to the new medium. Both being panel shows, the conversion was relatively

---

*An important factor in the success of IMH was a media plan that included a formidable block of prime time TV 10-second station identification spots which the brand owned and controlled, and sometimes temporarily leased to other B&B clients.

simple and economical. Ted Steele describes the transformation of *Meet the Press:*

"We stuck a couple of painted flats behind Lawrence Spivak (the permanent panelist) and moderator Martha Rountree, plunked a couple of cameras down in front of them and we had a television show. When we took the show to NBC, Frank Mullen, the program chief, didn't want to put it on because he thought Spivak was a 'Red.' When the show gained great popularity with its news-making guests —and high ratings—NBC changed its mind and bought the show from Rountree and Spivak for more than a million bucks."

There being no coaxial cables, the shows were broadcast live in New York and kinescopes—crude 16mm films made by photographing the image on the picture tube—were bicycled around to other stations.

Soon after the TV conversion of *Meet the Press,* the first coaxial cable was installed between New York and Washington, which allowed the show to originate in the nation's capital. On TV's first remote pickup, Spivak and Rountree had as their guest Senator Robert A. Taft, then an aspirant for the Republican presidential nomination. Other radio retreads in 1947 were two other panel shows, *Can You Top This?* with Harry Hershfield and Peter Donald, and *Leave It To The Girls,* featuring Dorothy Kilgallen, a popular Hearst gossip columnist.

The agency's first show produced especially for TV was an extravaganza called *Fashions on Parade,* sponsored by Ivory Snow and broadcast from the Dumont studio which occupied the auditorium of Wanamaker's department store at 8th Street and Broadway. As the name indicates, it was a fashion show with models parading before the camera. The commercials, featuring Julia Meade as a "stocking model," were more of the same. (Ivory Snow was then advertised for fine fabrics.) The whole thing, Frank Smith recalls with a shudder, "looked like a high-school play."

Steele, who presented the show to Bill Ramsey of P&G Productions, recalls the problem he had selling it: "Gil Ralston and Wyllis Cooper of Compton were at P&G the same day, trying to sell Ramsey *Fireside Theatre.* They vehemently argued that the future of television was film, not live. Not sure where TV was going, P&G ended up buying both shows."

Although film eventually became a primary source of TV programming, the Hollywood studios initially wanted nothing to do with the upstart medium, thinking (and hoping) the whole thing would go away. Robert Kintner, former head of ABC TV programming, recalled talking to Columbia's tyrannical president, Harry Cohn (reported in Max Wilk's *The Golden Age of Television):* "I remember he said something like, 'You dumb young son of a bitch, you won't get any of my stars, you won't get any people. *You* can't make films! People want the companionship of the theatre . . . they want their movies the way they *are,* not on TV!'"*

As a result of this Hollywood boycott, the networks and advertising agencies were forced to turn to other program sources—old Terry Tunes cartoons and ancient Grade B films, and importantly, live studio presentations. Some historians of the medium, including Wilk, say television's golden age was the era of live programming, from the late '40s to the mid-'50s, before videotape—the era of *Studio One, Kraft Theatre, Philco Playhouse,* the *Ford Television Theatre,* Sid Caesar and *Your Show of Shows, Garroway at Large, Mama.* Maybe so, says Kintner, but adds, "Those early shows . . . simply couldn't survive today. Film shows would knock them off very fast. (They) didn't have . . . dimension, movement—they were mostly talk." Eventually, TV programmers came to this view, and saw that to realize the full potential of the medium they had to break out of the confines of the studio into the action-packed world of film.

In the meantime, TV was mainly studio-bound, with the notable exception of Brooklyn Dodgers telecasts from Ebbets Field, and sports events from Madison Square Garden, a Saturday night staple that sent sports fans flocking to their local gin mills and ushered in the age of electronic sports and the TV widow.**

---

*Cohn and other Hollywood moguls proved to be lousy prophets. In 1975 NBC paid $15 million for the television rights to *Godfather* and *Godfather II.*

**There were only about 10,000 sets in 1947 in the metropolitan area (150,000 nationally), most of them, except for the tavern sets, owned by the well-to-do. When the agency got its first set—a 6-inch RCA Victor—the B&B Bulletin carried this notice: "Agency television representative Herb Leder has instructed Walter Craig, Ted Steele and Bill Vallee in the operation of the set and at present other members of the agency are not authorized to operate it."

Fashions on Parade was the first television show seen by P&G president Richard Deupree, who Smith said "was fascinated, particularly by the idea of TV as a demonstration medium."

Deupree's interest in the demonstration potential of television was destined to become an article of faith in P&G's commercial credo. Perhaps no other advertiser has used the technique with more telling effect. From the first simple visualization of the granulated form of Ivory Snow in the late '40s, to the demonstration of superior absorbency in current Pampers commercials, the "show-and-tell" sequence has been the centerpiece of most commercials for the company's brands.

In search of dramatic demonstrations, sometimes an earnest copywriter went overboard. In an early Drene shampoo commercial, a duck was washed in Drene to demonstrate the product's ability to remove oil from hair (in this case, feathers). When dropped into a tank of water, the very surprised duck *sinks*, and is scooped out only as it's about to go down for the third time.

The Lambs Gambol

> *"At these prices, we won't be able to stay in television."*
>
>> —General Foods client in 1949 upon hearing that the *Lambs Gambol* cost $15,000 a week.

To a client accustomed to paying $6,500 a week for *Showboat*, a top radio show and a full hour long, the tab on the agency's first big half hour TV variety show was "absolutely outrageous," as the GF representative put it.

The *Lambs Gambol*, produced in association with the Lambs Club, the famed men's theatrical organization that included most of the stars of stage, screen and radio, premiered February 27, 1949, live from NBC's Center Theatre, rechristened the Video Theatre. To publicize the show, sponsored by Maxwell House Coffee, B&B's PR department hired Jim Moran, professional screwball and self-styled "axiom-smasher." Moran, who had sold an icebox to an Eskimo, led a bull through a china shop and found a needle in a haystack, dreamed up a far more complicated caper for the show. Wearing a shepherd's cloak and leading an 80-pound lamb named Maxwell, he sat down in the middle of Times Square and played dice. "I've heard so much about the *Lambs Gambol,*" he told the gaping onlookers, "I wanted to find out just how good gamblers lambs are." A wag in the crowd, getting into the spirit of the thing, asked if Maxwell the lamb was "good to the last chop."

Despite the plethora of puns, the stunt had the desired effect: the story got into the gossip columns, including Winchell's.

As TV copywriter on the show, I remember the agony we all went through getting the first show on the air. The chief problem: nobody quite knew what he was doing. Everybody was a greenhorn in a strange new medium. Radio department head Walter Craig, the executive producer, had been a chorus boy in musical comedy, but television was playing a different tune; Tom McDermott had directed nothing more complicated than *Leave It to the Girls;* and I, lately of the NBC news department, had never written a TV commercial.

But what a cast I had to work with! That first live commercial featured musical comedy stars William Gaxton and Bobby Clark; Gene Tunney; Howard Chandler Christie, the noted illustrator; Hollywood actor Otto Krueger; and Fred Waring and his glee club. During rehearsal, as *Business Week* reported, "Waring, miffed, railed at his glee club, at the NBC technicians and the director. On the air, he buried his face in the script." (Out of sheer mortification, as I recall, a sentiment shared by most of us.)

"Is it worth it?" *Business Week* asked, giving a cost comparison between radio and TV: "At a cost of $15,000 a week its cost per listener is around 1½c on the basis of an audience of a million. A top radio show may reach 20 million at a cost per listener of 1/5c."

A lot of people at both the agency and GF asked the same question. They finally concluded that the *Lambs Gambol,* at least, was not worth the money. It was cancelled after seven weeks.

But there was no turning back. Despite the pain, the pratfalls and the price, the great engine of television was clattering into our lives, and nothing would ever be the same.

I Remember Mama

The next General Foods venture into television was a series about a Norwegian-American family, the Hansens, based on Katrin Forbes's best seller, *Mama's Bank Account*, which became a Broadway play by John Van Druten, *I Remember Mama*. Called simply *Mama*, it starred Peggy Wood in the title role. Judson Laire played Papa, Rosemary Rice Katin, Dick Van Patten Nels, and Dagmar was played by Robin Morgan (who grew up to be a poet and a leader in the women's lib movement).*

"Nobody at CBS ever really expected the show to be a success," Peggy Wood observed years later (reported in *The Golden Age of Television*). "One of the network bosses said, 'I give it a fast eight weeks.' We outlasted *him* by a good seven years."

Max Wilk, one of the writers on the show, remembers *Mama:* "They were gentle stories, somewhat old fashioned in their morality, certainly not related to the high-pressure standards of 'sitcoms' of today. . . ." The show "ended each week by everybody gathering in Mama's kitchen for a cup of freshly-brewed, good-to-the-last-drop Maxwell House coffee."

The commercials were integrated with the plot of the show (I wrote the commercials and, for five years, was one of the show writers), and were placed at the end of the program which played the full half hour without interruption. The absence of a middle break, as Peggy Wood pointed out, " . . . gave us a chance to build the story from beginning to end. . . . Once we had the audience involved, we didn't lose them. *Ever.*" This was borne out by audience profile surveys which showed that the audience level of the show remained constant for the half hour, even through the commercial.

The show family was almost like a real family. Birthdays of cast members, writers, producer Carol Irwin, script editor Frank Gabrielson and director Ralph Nelson, were celebrated family style. There was always a Christmas party, usually in the Lillian Russell room at Luchow's. One of the more endearing characters on the show

---

*A onetime member of the *Mama* cast was Al Stauderman who, before *he* grew up and became associate manager of P&G Productions, was a child actor and appeared on the show as Dagmar's boyfriend.

was T.R., played by seven-year-old Kevin Coughlin, who inadvertently caused a near-disaster on one show. I had written a script in which T.R., who had been living with the Hansens, was threatened with banishment to an orphanage. So real was the show family to young Kevin that he thought he really *was* going to be sent away from the family and the show. He did a fair amount of crying during the week's rehearsals, but when the program hit the air, the floodgates opened, and he bawled throughout the entire show, so hard he was wholly incoherent. At the last moment, he was reprieved—Mama's sister, Aunt Jenny, adopted him.

The show ran for eight years, until videotape brought an end to live drama.*

The pattern of agency-owned and -produced shows begun in radio continued in television. *Captain Video*, starring Al Hodges,** was not only created and produced by B&B, the props for it were built in the agency's art department. Other early agency-produced shows included *Pantomime Quiz*, and television's first daytime serial, *The First Hundred Years*, which lasted less than 1 percent as long as its title anticipated.

Although major Hollywood studios refused to make films available to TV, other sources did. William Boyd dusted off the negatives of his early film serial, *Hopalong Cassidy*, and launched a second, very profitable career. (The series was sponsored by, among others, Post Cereals.) Singing cowpokes Gene Autry and Roy Rogers saddled up and rode into the growing number of TV homes, dragging their money bags behind them. Rogers and his horse Trigger also starred in a number of rodeo "Specials" (a programming trend begun by B&B) produced for General Foods. (Other "Specials" included telecasts of the Barnum & Bailey circus and Jack Benny.)

The instant success of horse operas led, in 1955, to the development of the "adult western" which traded violence for vocal-

---

*One theory holds that there was quality drama during the live era because television in its early years was an elitist medium that appealed to a more affluent, better educated public—people who could afford the high cost of TV sets.

**Hodges, who was also the Green Hornet on radio, went into an eclipse after *Captain Video* left the air in 1956, ending his days as a security guard. He died in a Manhattan hotel room in 1979.

izing. *Wyatt Earp, Gunsmoke, Cheyenne* and *Bonanza* launched a shoot-'em-up era on the home screen that still echoes in the nostalgic memory of the television generation.

It wasn't all boots and saddle. From the beginning of TV, the agency and its first client, General Foods, had an affinity for family series and situation comedy. *Our Miss Brooks, Father Knows Best, December Bride,* the *Red Buttons Show,* the *Danny Thomas Show* had the humor and family warmth that General Foods felt provided a compatible environment for the advertising of family products. By now Tom McDermott, the Boy Wonder, was 37 and headed the radio-TV department, with Ted Steele as management supervisor of both programming and media. Ollie Barbour was director of programming and Larry White* program supervisor.

The highly successful *Danny Thomas Show* was a stunning coup for McDermott. Originally called *Make Room for Daddy,* it was languishing in 57th place on ABC, ready for oblivion. But McDermott believed in the star. Against resistance from just about everybody, he changed the format from a show business milieu to a family situation comedy, recast and renamed the show, and sold General Foods and CBS on it. In three weeks it was number one, and McDermott was something of a hero in agency and broadcasting circles. This feat of showmanship wasn't his first. In 1947 he originated *Wendy Warren and the News,* an innovative series that combined a news program with a daytime serial. McDermott also helped develop *Rawhide* and its spinoff, *The Rifleman,* the *Andy Griffith Show* (a spinoff of *Danny Thomas*), *Gomer Pyle* (an Andy Griffith spinoff), the *Loretta Young Show,* and Dick Powell's *Zane Grey Theatre,* the show that finally dislodged Walter Winchell from his top-rated spot. In 1959 McDermott joined Powell's company, Four Star Productions, as executive vice-president. He now heads his own production company.

The two B&B-produced daytime serials, *Edge of Night* and *As the World Turns* (both owned and sponsored by Procter & Gamble),

---

*White later moved to CBS where he was in charge of program development. Merle Miller in *Only You, Dick Daring* describes a meeting with White over a pilot Miller was writing, in which he marvels at White's mastery of the noncommittal head movement: "White moved (his head) in what might have been a nod. On the other hand it might have been a shake. Put it this way, no jury is ever going to convict White on a head-moving charge."

were also initiated during the McDermott regime. The first half-hour daytime serials on TV, they both premiered on the same day in April 1956. P&G, which had expanded the standard daytime format to accommodate their growing number of products, initially had serious doubts about the new length.

"Could we produce a half hour show every day with twice the number of sets and actors who had to learn twice as many lines?" asked Ed Trach of P&G Productions, in a historical review of P&G daytime shows for a P&G year-end sales meeting in 1975. And most important, "Would the audience sit still to watch a half hour serial every day?"

The answer was not long in coming. Audiences not only sat still, they loved the longer shows, and their devotion put *Edge* and *World* among the top-rated daytime serials. Although consistently high on the rating charts, *World* has had its slumps. During one such period, Irna Philips, creator of the series, was asked once again to script it. She decided the problem required major surgery, and eliminated several characters in what cast members remember as "the Monday Morning Massacre." One character, critically injured after a fall down a flight of stairs, was allowed to die, despite a flood of letters from concerned listeners, and the show had one of the most tearful funerals in its tear-filled history. Another character's wife was killed off to allow the husband to become involved in a romantic story line.

In 1975 *World* was expanded to an hour, which requires two complete production staffs. "It's a killing pace," says Art Richards, producer of the serial. "By the end of the day, I don't know my own name."

Nick Nicholson, *The Edge of Night*'s producer since 1966, calls the daytime serials " . . . the most consistently demanding area of the entire industry . . . it's not a place for people of weak heart or mind." His recipe for *Edge*'s daily dramatic concoction: "Take forty pages of lean, meaty dialogue; blend in seven versatile actors; combine these with one seasoned director; place in appropriate scenery; add lighting; simmer for six hours; sprinkle with wardrobe, make-up and hair styling. Serves about six million."

By 1979 P&G had five daytime serials, three of them one hour in length, which accounted for some one thousand hours of family triumph and tragedy a year, more hours of programs than all the feature films produced in Hollywood in an average year.

"More than radio with pictures"

Creative director "Pat" Pattison had a staff of some fifteen radio copywriters in 1948, and twice that number in print. "But I had a feeling" he said recently, "that television was more than radio with pictures, that it was going to need a different kind of talent. So I talked to some people in film I knew, and got the names of some film-trained writers and art people."

That's how I came into the B&B story.

Pattison hired me on the recommendation of radio copy head Ed Mead, largely on the basis of my background as writer for the first anchorman in TVnews, John Cameron Swayze, on the NBC *Television Newsreel*. Two industrial film companies yielded two other TV tyros—Ray Lind, who'd been an animator at Audio Productions, and Wes Emmart, an artist with Transfilm. Ed Mahony, an artist with a smattering of film experience, came, of all places, from the State Department. And Tom Dunphy hove in from Hollywood where his film career had been given a boost by an uncle, the longtime manager of W.C. Fields. Another early member of the TV group was Len McKenzie, who wrote most of the agency's jingles from 1947 to 1956.

That was the B&B TV department *circa* 1948–50. None of us knew much about advertising, and some of us damned little about film. (When Pattison asked me "Do you work with storyboards?", I finessed the question until I could ask Lind what the hell a storyboard was.)

And, of course, we knew nothing about television. But nobody else did, either. So we were left on our own to invent, to improvise and make it up as we went along. The main action—and billings—was still in print and radio, with television, in 1949, accounting for only about 4 percent of that year's billings of $39 million.

Partly because of Ray Lind's background in animation, partly because the few people commercials we'd made turned out so badly (how could you get live actors to do what you wanted?), a lot of the early commercials by the team of McKenzie-Lind-Webber were animated. The first spot we did—the first fully animated 60-second spot on TV—was for Post Toasties. Jack Zander of Transfilm produced it. When I asked him what it would cost, he said, "Gee, I don't know. Never did one before. Would $1,700 be too much?" (He learned fast. The next spot cost $4,500.)

The sudden appearance of this group of disparate types in the agency's creative department caused a lot of speculation and some suspicion. My first office was a glass cubicle off the bull pen, and the artists became convinced, Bill Tompkins said, "that you were an efficiency expert, spying on them to see when they went out for coffee." When office space became tight, the whole gang of us was exiled to a suite in the New Weston Hotel* across the street from 444 Madison—a fortuitous move for me, since in the stress of mastering a new medium, I had slipped a disc in my lower back, and was able to write my commercials while sitting in a tub of hot water.

Len McKenzie began his career at BBDO where he wrote one of radio's early jingle classics, *Chiquita Banana*, for United Fruit. He recently recalled the initial reception of the jingle:

"Bob Foreman, my copy boss, and I were summoned to Bruce Barton's office. Barton said, 'It isn't dignified enough.' The account man said it was 'OK, but it isn't any Pepsi Cola.' The ad manager was cool to it, but they finally agreed to run it on a trial basis. When the chairman of United Fruit heard it, he said, 'Get that trash off the air!' But by this time they had such strong favorable feedback, they put it back on. When it became a big hit—Gene Krupa and Xavier Cugat recorded it and sold 600,000 records—the ad manager began to love it. He got drunk one night at the Stork Club, climbed on a table and sang *Chiquita*, modestly admitting that he had written it. Years later someone told me that on his deathbed his last words were, 'Well, at least I gave the world *Chiquita Banana*.' "

---

*The New Weston bar was a favorite watering hole (along with Cherio's and Finland House) of agency people in the '40s and '50s. When it was razed in the early '60s, one New Weston habitué mourned, "Ah, they're tearing down the best martini in town."

McKenzie, a talented musician who eventually went into business for himself, wrote jingles for Pepto-Bismol, Ivory Snow, Hellmann's Mayonnaise and many Post cereals, including one for Sugar Crisp which featured the lively antics of the three Sugar Crisp Bears. Following the successful *Chiquita* formula, he created Maisie the Raisin and Jake the Flake for Post Raisin Bran, and for Prell Concentrate shampoo a sultry-voiced character called "Tallulah, the Tube of Prell" that involved the agency and client in a much-publicized lawsuit. "Gil" Gilbert recently recalled the incident: "When the agency asked me if I thought Tallulah Bankhead would sue, I said, it's possible, but go ahead anyway, the publicity will be worth it."

Miss Bankhead lost no time. Shortly after the jingle hit the air, she sued Benton & Bowles and Procter & Gamble for $500,000 and the story made the front page of *The New York Times. Life* magazine ran a two-page spread, and the columnists kept the pot boiling. After weeks of negotiations, Gilbert finally settled with Miss Bankhead's lawyers for $7,000, with both parties tickled pink over the publicity.

"Is he in the book?"

In 1951, writes Robert Metz in *CBS: Reflections in a Bloodshot Eye*, Fred Friendly visited a CBS vice-president to request funds for hiring a composer to write music for *See It Now*. When the vice-president asked him what composers he had in mind, Friendly handed him a list of three names. The vice-president looked at the top name and asked, "Is he in the book?"

Friendly said he didn't know and asked for a telephone directory, "whereupon the vice-president reached in his desk, pulled out a copy of *Red Channels* and said, 'This is the book we live by.' "

It was the book most network and agency executives lived by during the blacklist era.

Red Channels and the weekly newsletter *Counterattack* were published by American Business Consultants, Inc., a backroom organization run by Theodore C. Kirkpatrick, a former FBI agent and Bloomingdale's security man, and Alfred Kohlberg, an importer. Their purpose was to alert broadcasters, advertisers and advertising agencies to what they called the dangers of communist "infiltration" by actors, directors and writers working in radio and television whom they presumably had investigated and found to be members of communist "front" organizations. (*Red Channels* listed 151 people with what the authors called "citations.") A product of the cold war, along with McCarthyism, the blacklist, as Erik Barnouw writes in *The Golden Web*, " . . . scarred many who clung to jobs, along with others who could not." The careers of many talented—and unjustly accused—people in the entertainment field were ruined. Some never worked again in their profession. At least one actor—Philip Loeb, who played Jake in *The Goldbergs* and was blacklisted—committed suicide.

The record of the advertising, broadcasting and business community as a whole during this period is not commendable. Almost everybody, while deploring the blacklist and the police state mentality behind it, routinely consulted "the book" before hiring performers, writers and directors. But there was at least one attempt to combat it by two advertising agencies and a major client in 1952. In a joint meeting between producers, the Radio Writers Guild and representatives of Compton, Benton & Bowles and Procter & Gamble,* a resolution was signed which said, in part: "It is the unanimous belief of this . . . Board that blacklisting in *any* field is destructive to good labor-management relations, and therefore (we) recommend to the several signatories to the Producers and Radio Writers Guild Agreement that they join with each other in issuing a statement declaring such opposition."

It was a brave public stand, but the only result was an attack by *Counterattack* on the people who signed the resolution and their companies.

Only with the decline and eventual downfall of McCarthy did the era of vigilantism end. It left many with scars, and many more with a sense of shame.

---

*The representatives included Leonard Bush for Compton; William Schneider for Benton & Bowles; and William F. Ramsey for Procter & Gamble.

"We've decided to run your damned coupons"

To put muscle and sinew on the merchandising leg of his "Triangle of Marketing Success," in 1952 Hobler asked Austin Johnson to set up a merchandising department. Johnson, who headed the store audit group of research, lost no time in assembling a small cadre of promotion experts, including Bill Noble, now head of the department, which during the next 25 years provided a service to clients in promotion planning and developing of merchandising ideas.

Among the more successful promotions dreamed up by Johnson and his crew: a reusable carafe packed with Instant Maxwell House coffee (11 million were sold); a waste basket packed with Tide; "sprinkle sampling" for Johnson's Pledge—a new wrinkle in sampling in which one house in twenty received mailings; a contest for Conoco that offered a Cadillac full of cash; and the Hardee Fun Machine that dispensed kiddie premiums in the chain's food shops, called by a promotion industry spokesman "the first really new promo idea in ten years."

Johnson, now retired to Florida after 27 years at B&B, recalls a meeting with Hobler on promotion plans for the Florida Citrus Commission which had promised the agency an extra $5 million to help move a glut of product off the shelves before the new orange crop came in, if they could come up with a plan:

"I argued for an hour that we should blanket the country with 50 million 10c-off coupons. Hobe wanted cash refunds. I said, 'Hobe, refunds aren't strong enough.' (They required the customer to mail in proof of purchases instead of getting 10c off at the store.) Hobe hit the desk with his hand so hard, one of our guys jumped a foot off his chair, and said, 'Dammit, Austin, I want it done my way!' But the next morning he called and said, 'All right. We've decided to run your damned coupons.' When we made the presentation to the Commission—after rehearsing all one Sunday—Hobe got up to introduce the agency team, and didn't stop—made the entire presentation hmself! Afterwards, he said, 'I'm sorry, but it was going so well, I decided to keep going.'"

New Business Bonanza

> *"Every advertising agency is like a leaky bucket. You have to keep pouring it in at the top, or one day you'll find yourself empty."*
>
> —Charlie Brower, *Me and Other Advertising Geniuses*

The detergent decade was also the decade of the big ducats for the agency, as new product assignments poured in from clients new and old.

Billings increased more than four-fold, from about $22 million in 1946 to $90 million in 1956. A sizable amount of this increase came from existing clients, always an important source of growth in the agency's history.* Tide's phenomenal success alone accounted for more than $11 million in annual billings by 1956. Other new assignments from old clients included Yuban coffee from General Foods, and from Procter & Gamble, Crest toothpaste, a product that would upset the status quo of the dentifrice world as dramatically as Tide had upset the laundry product field.

The frenetic new medium of television, more than anything else, was the catalyst, the stimulator, of the postwar decade. Its unique sight-and-sound communicative force revved up the tempo of life wherever it reached, and it reached into the lives of more people with every passing month. By 1955 there were 37 million TV sets in the U.S. It created, with its closeups, its demonstrations, its overpowering intimacy, an "I-want-that" hunger that accelerated the marketing of new products. Contrary to Marshall McLuhan's theory of a few years later that television was a "cool" medium, as far as its *advertising* force was concerned, television was hotter than a two-dollar pistol.

The agency's preeminence in the broadcast field—specifically television—certainly was no obstacle to its quest for new business. In

---

*A house ad appearing in 1951 stated: "Since 1941, over 50 percent of (our) yearly increase has come from existing clients in expanding campaigns and in new assignments."

the ten-year period following the war, 28 new clients assigned products to B&B. Three of them, Kinsey Distilling Corp., Time Inc. and Whitehall Laboratories, were in and out in the same year. But most of the others established longer relationships. These included American Express, Mutual Insurance Company of New York, Carling Brewing Company (Red Cap ale), Philip Morris (Benson & Hedges and Parliament), International Business Machines,* Continental Oil, the Florida Citrus Commission (for the second time**), Studebaker Corporation, and two companies that are still clients after 35 and 30 years, respectively, Norwich Pharmacal (now Norwich-Morton), and S. C. Johnson Company.

The decade of growth had its setbacks and losses. The Can Manufacturers Institute picked up its marbles and left. *American Magazine* and the Bituminous Coal Institute left. Three accounts were resigned by Hobler: Schenley Distillers, because the client representative, in Hobler's words, "insulted and swore at the agency's account people." Best Foods was resigned, regretfully, after twenty years, because the agency and client couldn't agree on a marketing recommendation. And the agency parted company with Arnold Bakers over *l'affaire boxing gloves*. A former agency executive recalls the incident:

"Dean Arnold kept sending Hobe these little locker-room pep talks. One week it was a miniature baseball bat with a card reading, 'Expect a home run with that new TV series!' (*The Faye Emerson Show.*) Another time it was a football with the message, 'I want a touchdown every time out!' The day a small pair of boxing gloves arrived with a tag reading, 'Let's get more punch into our copy!' Hobe called the game on account of clichés, and resigned the account."

---

*In an early solicitation of IBM, Hobler asked account supervisor Jack Reeder to call on IBM board chairman Tom Watson. Sensitive to some prospective clients' criticism of the agency's original partners because of their politics, he told Reeder: "Reassure Watson that Bill Benton and Chet Bowles no longer have any connection with B&B." Reeder said, "But Tom Watson is a Democrat." "Well, in that case," said Hobler, "Tell him they're still very much involved with the business."

**The man in charge of the agency's office in Lakeland, Florida, servicing the Citrus account, was Harry Warren, a dark-haired, affable, smartly dressed man with a penchant for French wines and foreign sports cars. When Hobler sent him down to Florida, Warren had to get rid of his cherished XK120 Jaguar roadster and "dress down" a bit, because Hobler was afraid the citrus farmers on the Commission would think he was "too high-toned."

In the June 1950 B&B Bulletin, this item appeared: "A newcomer to the 8th floor is Victor Bloede who arrived June 19 to be a copywriter in Cap Billip's* group. . . . Victor is still breathless from complications of moving into a new house in Roslyn."

When Bloede went to work on the Railroad account, there was no indication (no flags were put out, no bugles sounded) that eighteen years later he would step into the presidency at a critical time in the agency's history, the first creative person to assume the title, and begin to shape a "new" Benton & Bowles. It was certainly far from Bloede's thoughts.

"Hobe tells a story in his autobiography," he says, "about my being asked shortly after Pattison hired me what I eventually wanted to be. Hobe reports that I said, 'President,' but I think the story is apocryphal. All I wanted to be at the time was just a damned good copywriter."

Victor Gustav Bloede, a six-foot-two, quiet-spoken native of Maryland, attended the University of Maryland and St. Johns College (where he is now on the board of governors), and wanted to be a writer from an early age. His first mentor was Henry Hough, author of the best-selling *Country Editor*, and editor of the *Vineyard Gazette* where Bloede worked as a reporter during summer vacations. Drafted into the Army, he trained in Texas, met his future wife, Mickey Huie, there, and rose to captain in the 8th Air Force based in England. As a B-17 bombardier he flew 33 missions, and was decorated with the Air Medal with six oak-leaf clusters. One of his missions was the bombing of Dresden, which gave a special relevance, he says, to his reading of Kurt Vonnegut's *Slaughterhouse-Five*.

After the war he went to work as a publicity writer with Young & Meyers, the PR firm started by John Orr Young, cofounder of Young & Rubicam, a job that included writing ads for certain clients. Young spotted some of the ads and told Bloede, "Maybe your real career lies in advertising." Following Young's suggestion, Bloede switched to French & Preston, where he eventually became copy

---

*Billip, a crusty, colorful advertising pro with crew haircut and a game leg, worked on Mutual Life Insurance of New York. It was his idea to change the company's name to its present form, MONY ("Money" without the "E").

chief. "This meant," Bloede said, "that I could take my own copy to the clients, but I didn't have any writers under me."

One of his first Railroad Association assignments, Bloede recalls, was a trip from New York to Chicago—riding in the caboose of a freight train. "Ralph Seberhagen the art director and Bill Foxen the account man went along, too. Longest, boringest trip I ever made," Bloede says. "We were supposed to return by train, but I'd had enough of trains and we came back by plane instead. John Cobb, the supervisor on the account was horrified, afraid the client would find out!"

Another early assignment was the Bituminous Coal Institute which, Bloede says, inevitably inspired new copywriters to write, as their first headline, "There's No Fuel Like an Old Fuel."

The advertising business was a lot more relaxed in those pre-television days, he says. "You wrote your two or three ads for the month, then waited for your next assignment. Doc Hubbell, who wrote dealer ads—every ad he wrote, I remember, featured either an explosion or an arrow—had invented a word game, and we spent our down time playing that. Another harmless diversion was the WICS, the Wild Cat Investment Club. A group of us—Doc, Paul Podgus, John Flagg and Bill Benner (copywriters), Dick Sutter, Jean Finnegan, Bill Stillwell, Gordon Ensign, Dave Donovan, Dale Strand, Bruce Allen and Quent McDonald* (account men), used to have lunch every Friday at Cherio's and bet on football games. During off-seasons we invested in stocks. After twenty-five years a few survivors—Doc, Dave, Bill Stillwell and Gordon are dead—still meet during the football season."

The private-to-captain progression of Bloede's Army career was repeated at Benton & Bowles. He soon became a group head, and in 1955 was made copy supervisor and elected a vice-president. (No time for Doc's word game now.) Originally an expert in writing "issues" advertising for the agency's association clients, he soon moved into consumer products. Among the assignments under his wing

---

*McDonald resigned from the agency in 1967 and set up a company to manufacture and distribute an invention of his, the Bobby-Mac baby chair, and eventually became a client of B&B. An ad for the Bobby-Mac, written by veteran copywriter Bob Povey, has run unchanged for eight years.

were Crosley ("A Carefree Kitchen is the Heart of the Home"); American Express ("Never Carry More Cash Than You Can Afford to Lose"); Conoco ("Hottest Brand Going"); Harvey's Bristol Cream ("Never Serve the Coffee Without the Cream"); IBM and Post Cereals. He was later to work on Parliament ("The Most Important ¼-Inch in Smoking Today"); and Texaco, for which he wrote the famous slogan, "You Can Trust Your Car to the Man Who Wears the Star."

Bloede also worked on some of the last advertising for Studebaker. They were a difficult client, Bloede recalls.

"We had a lot of trouble selling them anything. I remember one especially painful meeting. They came into our office one morning still bleary-eyed from a night on the town, and weaved over to the wall where we had the layouts tacked up. They studied them in boozy silence for a long time. Then one man turned to the other and said, 'C'mon, let's go. There ain't anything here that could sell call girls in a lumber camp!'* And they walked out. I felt terrible, of course. But the next day they came back, sober, and bought the whole campaign."

A Death In The Family

On December 11, 1950, Atherton Hobler wrote a memorandum to the organization which read, in part:

> Our dear Clarence Goshorn passed away last evening due to accidental death by drowning. . . . You can appreciate how impossible it is for me to attempt to express at this time our feeling about this tragedy, for Clarence has meant so much to all of us . . . not only as a leader, but also as a friend and a member of our family.

Goshorn had been attending a coffee conference in Florida, and had sailed on a friend's yacht, the *Golden Fleece*, to Bimini where he tripped and fell from a dock into the water.

The agency closed its offices the Friday before Christmas so that the employees could, in the words of the Bulletin announcement,

---

*This being a family book, this phrase has been sanitized.

"in the quiet of our homes and hearts, give to Clarence's memory a day that would normally be spent in seasonal office revelry."*

Goshorn, president since 1942, had been named chairman of the board six months before his death, with Hobler moving to chairman of the executive committee, a title new to the industry, devised by Gilbert. Now Hobler reassumed the chairmanship, Bill Baker was named president and Bob Lusk executive vice-president, Hobler still remaining firmly in charge. In 1954 Baker became chairman and Lusk president, a prelude to the time, two years later, when Hobler would step down and Lusk would become chief executive officer.

The end of an era was approaching. Hobler, now 65, had decided it was time to relax a measure of his control over the agency he had guided, day by day, for more than twenty years.

At least that was the intention. Just how much control this benevolent, despotic "father" would be willing to relinquish over his extended "family"—a family he loved as fiercely as his real family, or his cherished Guernsey cows—remained to be seen.

---

*The origin of the custom, continued to this day, that B&B does not have an office party at Christmas.

Six

"It was the best of times,
it was the worst of times."
1956–61

"*I* am increasingly concerned and very much annoyed," wrote Bob Lusk in *Broadcasting* early in 1958 by critics who give "false impressions about advertising. These half-truths persist and grow every time some novelist feels the need to 'jazz up' his work, filling it with . . . cheats, glib charlatans and eccentrics, depicting them as typical advertising people."

Three years later, Lusk was very much annoyed by another critic of advertising, the agency's cofounder, Chester Bowles. Bowles, on a CBS interview program, had said advertising and public life "are a million miles apart," and that the best thing an advertising man wanting to get into public life can do is leave the advertising business. In a *New York Herald-Tribune* front-page story, Lusk rebuked Bowles for being as guilty of "exaggeration" as he claimed the advertising business was. To Bowles's statement that "if I were doing it over again, I would have gone into government immediately after college," Lusk said, "I am disturbed about the effect his comments may have on our young people who are deciding on careers today. . . . It is ridiculous for any successful businessman to make remarks about any other business, including advertising, and I am disappointed in Mr. Bowles for having done so." The story sparked widespread comment in the industry, including an angry editorial in *Advertising Age* attacking both Bowles and Bill Benton for taking pot shots at advertising, and suggesting that "maybe a change in name for the agency might finally be called for."

Lusk became chief executive officer in July 1956, in the midst of a period of vigorous growth and prosperity for the agency. Flexing his new-found managerial muscles, he took a statesmanlike stance and decided it was time somebody did something about improving advertising's image. The result was the agency's first major house campaign, a series of ads in the *Wall Street Journal* aimed at dispelling "common misunderstandings about advertising." One ad featured a cartoon by Peter Arno of two old geezers lazing under a beach umbrella with their drinks, with the caption, "Trouble is, J.B., advertising makes people *buy* things they don't *need!*"

There is no evidence that the campaign changed the public's attitude toward advertising—a problem that has worried the industry for most of its history, and probably has been further exacerbated by the high visibility of its product on television. But the campaign was an indication of the affluence the agency was enjoying as, in that year, it passed the magic $100-million billing mark. Only an agency that had "arrived" could afford the luxury of such philosophic reflection.

Increasingly conscious of its statesman's role, the agency prepared and distributed during this period two industry "White Papers": a study of economic turndowns since 1897 (the country was in the midst of one at the time) designed to show that "recessions are historically short-lived affairs which produce more discussion than damage;" and a study of marketing opportunities in Alaska, written by copywriter John Flagg after he and account executive Ben Davis visited the new 49th state. Both studies made a modest splash in the business press (*Advertising Age* headlined the first: "B&B Pooh-Poohs Recession; Says It Will Go Away"), and were part of an effort by Lusk and others in top management to project a more distinctive profile for the agency, which for more than twenty years had labored, and prospered, in relative anonymity behind Atherton Hobler's personality. Although brilliantly effective in a one-to-one relationship with clients and his colleagues, Hobler was not a good speaker in public nor, at any time, a very articulate man. Lusk, on the other hand, was a forceful, eloquent speaker, a person of both elegance and warmth who, as one former associate said, "could charm the birds out of the trees."

Having reached a new high in billings, the agency decided in

1958 that it should set its sights even higher. "Benton & Bowles, with billings of $100 million," wrote Martin Mayer in *Madison Avenue, USA*, "has made the executive decision that it is too small . . . (and) must go to $150 million before (it) can consider itself 'safe.'" (It would briefly reach that goal eight years later, only to fall back to lower levels for several years during a time of reversals.)

The stage was set for growth. On the weekend before Christmas 1957, the one thousand members of the B&B family packed up their typewriters and T-squares, their pictures and potted plants, and moved into quarters in the new aluminum-facaded Tishman Building at 666 Fifth Avenue. The functionally modern building was nothing fancy, despite a lobby designed by Noguchi. A current joke had it that it was the packing case the Seagram Building came in. Martin Mayer wrote that "such giants as Batten, Barton, Durstine & Osborn (and) Benton & Bowles . . . have snuggled into office settings so nondescript or old shoe that a high-class accountant would scorn them as insufficiently stylish."

But the new digs suited the aggressive, no-nonsense Lusk regime. In the next half decade under his suave, professional stewardship, some sixteen new accounts were added to the agency's roster, and as many new assignments from existing clients. Schick came to the agency with a major new product development—a three-speed electric razor. Hobler, still very much in the picture, was management supervisor. Other new clients included Kentile, Chemical Bank of New York, Shulton, Glass Container Manufacturers Institute, and in 1961 a major acquisition, Texaco, which at the time was under the firm leadership of Gus Long.*

The agency had had its eye on Texaco for many years. In a memo dated May 18, 1939, Chet Bowles wrote Hobler: "I wonder how long Texaco . . . will struggle along with 'Star Theatre.' 11.8

---

*Helen Scofield, Lusk's secretary for twenty years, recalls the tension of waiting to hear whether the agency had gotten the account. "Bob never left his office all week, waiting to hear from John Childs (Texaco advertising manager). He finally left early on Friday afternoon—it was the Fourth of July weekend—and the moment he walked out, the call came—and nobody was there to take it! We got the account anyway."

Childs remembers that Benton & Bowles almost didn't get the account. "Gus Long had assumed our choice was J. Walter Thompson. When I met with him that Friday afternoon, he said, 'Now, if you go with Thompson, you don't have to take all their foreign offices.' I told him my choice was Benton & Bowles. He seemed surprised, but went along with it."

(Crossley rating) sounds pretty terrible and they must think so too. I wonder if a call from you on some of the boys down there might not ring the bell about now."

Hands Across the Sea

Bob Lusk, for all his aggressive pursuit of new acquisitions domestically, was a conservative man when it came to international expansion. By the mid-'50s many major U.S. agencies had affiliations abroad. Only in 1958, partly due to the nudging of its major client, Procter & Gamble, did the agency stick a cautious toe into international waters. After a long courtship with Lambe & Robinson, Ltd., which had the P&G business in England, a union was consummated with the purchase of a majority interest in the London agency. The new affiliate, renamed Lambe & Robinson—Benton & Bowles, was under the supervision of Ed Murtfeldt in New York (and later Chick Pooler), and the New York representative in London was George Beaumont, later replaced by Townsend Griffin, who eventually became managing director.

It was the agency's first foreign venture, and initially so unpromising as a profit center that Lusk shied away from further international partnerships. It wasn't until 1966 that international expansion began in earnest with moves to Canada and Belgium, and eventually to a dozen other countries in Europe, North and South America. Under the generalship of Ted Steele, and later Vic Bloede, B&B's growth overseas would, by 1978, place it among the major international agencies in the world.

"I've got a million bucks to spend in a week. Let's go!"

When Dr. Joseph C. Muhler first began his experiments with fluoride in a toothpaste, he was still an undergraduate at the University of Indiana, and had to peddle newspapers at dawn to make ends meet.

That was in 1945. Eleven long years later, Crest toothpaste

with the stannous fluoride formula Dr. Muhler developed in collaboration with Procter & Gamble research scientists, was introduced by Benton & Bowles with the apocalyptic announcement:

TRIUMPH OVER TOOTH DECAY

With long, ethical copy written by Jerry Gury and John Jackson, and two-page spreads in *Life*, the campaign was launched with great expectations. But despite the revolutionary formulation and subsequent advertising featuring tests of Bloomington, Indiana, school children that showed Crest reduced cavities, the brand did not become the world-beater the client and agency had hoped it would. After four years of steady growth, it was still number three behind Colgate and P&G's own Gleem.

Then on August 1, 1960, the nation's press carried the news that the Council on Dental Therapeutics of the American Dental Association had endorsed Crest as "an effective decay-preventive dentifrice." The news sent Procter & Gamble's stock up 13½ points. *Time, Newsweek* and the *Wall Street Journal* carried long stories, and Crest entered a whole new phase of development. With the solid gold ADA endorsement—no other toothpaste would have it for five years—memorable advertising (Crest testers and "Look, Mom, No Cavities"), and an ever-growing advertising budget, Crest climbed steadily, finally displacing Colgate as the number one brand. For Atherton Hobler, watching closely from the sidelines, "Triumph Over Colgate" was an especially sweet victory, coming as it did twenty years after the great Bates/Colgate defection.

"Those were exciting times," recalls Jack Bowen, then the account executive on Crest. "We had dough to spend, we had consumer acceptance, and we were piling on the coal. John Smale was associate advertising manager and I worked closely with him. I'd be on the phone to John, Lee Rich would be on the phone with Jim Aubrey, CBS president, buying TV specials, buying spots, buying everything we could get our hands on. Rich invented what he called the 'scatter plan'—he bought up all the so-called garbage of the networks, anything that was available, very cheap. I'd walk into Rich's office and say, 'I've got a million bucks to spend in a week. Let's go!' And we took the brand to glory!"

For John Sheets Bowen, working on a Procter & Gamble assignment was as if he'd never left home. Six-foot-one and "handsome enough to be an actor," as a *New Yorker* article on Crest described him, Bowen was hired by P&G on the campus of Yale which he attended on a working scholarship, graduating in 3½ years, in 1949. His first assignment was calling on retail stores in the Italian section of Waterbury, Connecticut. "I bumped my head on more hanging cheeses," he says. His district manager, he remembers, was a tough taskmaster named Curran who would either "make you or break you." He successfully passed the Curran course, and within a few months was training new recruits himself, one of whom was Jim Cochran, later manager of P&G Productions.

"I played a mean trick on Jim once," Bowen recalls. "It was during the Korean war, and I got this telegram from Curran: 'Forget about training Cochran. Fats and oils going up. Bull the market'—that is, sell all you can before the price rise. So I did. I sold a ton of soap and Crisco. Then what happened was the brands were put on allocation, and most of the orders couldn't be shipped at the old prices. So Cochran had to go around and say to his customers, 'You remember that sonofabitch who sold you all that soap? Well, you ain't going to get it—it's on allocation.' It was a long time before Jim forgot that one!"

Bowen, like Bill Baker, began early in the grocery business—in Bowen's case, as a delivery boy and clerk at Wright & Irish groceries in his hometown of Scarsdale, New York. ("Brightest kid I ever had working for me," says Tom Irish.) His interest in advertising was first sparked by Young & Rubicam's Sig Larmon who lived across the street from his family, and by another neighbor, a Compton executive. "Both of them advised me to get some sales experience before going into advertising," he recalls. In 1952, after three years with P&G and marriage to Leigh Stander, he joined McCann-Erickson as a management trainee. After a year in the New York office, he was assigned to the Boston office where he found himself working on new business and making "a hell of a lot of cold calls. I was not only young and inexperienced," he says, "I was a Yalie, and those old Harvard guys hated Yalies." Back in the agency's New York office, he worked on the Savings and Loan Association and Esso accounts. "But I was hankering to get back to packaged goods," he says. When Marion Harper, McCann president and chairman of the board said "No" to this idea, Bowen resigned and came to Benton & Bowles. Bob Lusk sized him up and later said to a colleague, "I'm going to take a chance on this guy and see if he's as smart as I think he is." Ed Murtfeldt saw him and said, "I think you'll fit in here—but you're going to need some retraining."

He got the retraining under Bob Wallace, head of the marketing department, but soon got bored with charts and research reports and yearned for an account assignment. He called Murtfeldt and said, "I'm going nuts up here—I want to get into the fray."

He was made account executive on Prell, under account supervisor Bob Young* , and a year later moved to Crest. Once Bowen "got into the fray," he never stopped, moving steadily through vice-president, senior vice-president and management supervisor, executive vice-president in charge of account management, president and, in 1974, chief executive officer—a progression that wouldn't surprise his old employer, Tom Irish, one bit.

50 percent of All New Products Fail.
At Benton & Bowles 90 percent Succeed.

More than 1,000 food and drug products are introduced in the United States every year. According to the *Wall Street Journal* as many as half of them fail.

Happily for its clients, B&B's record of wins has been considerably better than the morning-line odds. In the period 1946–59, B&B launched 36 new products. Of these, sixteen climbed to first place in their product categories, and twelve were either second or third in their fields.

---

*Now president of *Family Circle*.

The strategy behind this record of success was boiled down in a house ad written by Vic Bloede to five questions an advertiser and his agency should ask before deciding if a product is ready for market:

1. Does the product have a perceivable superiority or difference?
2. Is the product positioned against the right segment of the market?
3. Does the advertising present the product as fulfilling a real need or desire?
4. Does the advertising communicate the selling idea clearly and memorably?
5. Does the product live up to what is claimed for it?

Of the half dozen new products launched during the last half of the '50s—among them Crest, Zest, Glade, Charmin and Gravy Train—no product more classically fulfilled these criteria, and enjoyed a more spectacular success, than Johnson's Pledge.

The agency's long association with the S. C. Johnson Company began in 1955 some three years before the introduction of Pledge, with the assignment of Jubilee and Paste Wax, and a year later, Beautiflor. Jim Haines, a copywriter at the time, recalls one of the first copy presentations to the new client at their Frank Lloyd Wright-designed headquarters in Racine, Wisconsin:

"I was presenting a commercial in front of a pyramid of empty Beautiflor cans and I was feeling pretty nervous because Mr. H. C. Johnson himself was in the audience. The old gentleman was hard of hearing and I was told I could gauge how I was doing by watching him: If he turned down the volume on his hearing aid, I was losing his interest. So I launched into my spiel and was doing fine until I saw Mr. Johnson fiddling with his dial. I got so flustered that I backed into the pile of cans and sent them tumbling with a godawful clatter. This so startled Mr. J—he'd turned his volume *up* instead of down—that he got up and stalked out, holding his ears."

The association survived the shambles of that clamorous meeting, and the trek to Johnson's—a flight to Milwaukee and a rental car to Racine—became a routine part of many of our lives. But a trip some half dozen of us* made in the summer of 1957 was anything but routine. Doug Smith, advertising manager, Ralph Deihl, brand manager, and their associates said they had an interesting new product they wanted to show us. And, they were frank to admit, they didn't quite know what to do with it.

The product was something eventually called Pledge—a water-based furniture polish in an aerosol can. At least that's what they thought they had. As we all sat around a long table, and a can of the new product was passed around, Ed Murtfeldt studied it a long time, squirted some on the surface of the table and wiped it up. Struck by how easy and fast the product produced a shine, he said, "It's as easy as dusting. What you've got here is not a furniture polish, but a *dusting wax*."

Nobody had ever heard of a dusting wax, but that is what it became, a whole new way to care for furniture. With the furniture polish field overcrowded, and declining in sales to boot, the agency decided to create an entirely new market category—a product that gave the housewife, in Liz Eddy's felicitous phrase, "waxed beauty instantly as you dust."

When blind tests showed that women preferred Pledge 6 to 1 over the best-selling furniture polish, and tended to use it daily rather than once a week as they did polishes, Johnson and the agency began to think they might have a winner.

Skipping the usual test market phase in order to get the jump on competition, Pledge was introduced in April of 1958, and by the end of the year had captured 50 percent of the furniture polish market.

The man whose innovative concept eventually changed the furniture care habits of the Western world was a gentle, balding, scholarly man (he once quit advertising to earn an M.A. in English at Columbia), whose favorite spot on earth was his "Heart K" ranch outside Livingston, Montana. Ed Murtfeldt came to Benton & Bowles in 1947, first as an account supervisor on Ivory Snow, Tide, Zest and

---

*Those attending for the agency included Bob Lusk, Ed Murtfeldt, Buck Weaver (account executive), Betty Pike and Liz Eddy (copy) and Ruth Ziff (research).

Camay, then as management supervisor on a group of accounts, including Johnson's Wax. He was elected executive vice-president in 1961, and could have gone on to be president.

"Lusk wanted him to take the job," Jack Bowen remembers. "But Murtfeldt said he didn't want it. 'I don't want to be out in front that much,' he told me. 'I plan to retire when I'm sixty and spend more time on my ranch. Besides, I don't want to have to do the things a president has to do.' But just the same, Ed was a power behind the throne. Lusk came to him on every important decision. He was the intellectual glue that held the company together, the man who typified the B&B character at its best."

Murtfeldt didn't reach retirement. In the spring of 1964, while playing paddle tennis, he collapsed and died, at a time, it turned out, when the agency most needed his wise counsel. He was 56.*

Some products, like Pledge, make it to the top in one giant leap. Others, like Zest, don't have it that easy. Originally test-marketed in 1954, Zest quickly reached leadership position, then declined alarmingly. Atherton Hobler, measuring the problem against his trusty marketing triangle, decided "the difficulty was not . . . in the area of advertising or merchandising (but) in the product quality side of the triangle." With the deodorant soap market rising, he felt Zest was at a competitive disadvantage, particularly against Armour and Company's Dial. He began to press P&G to add a deodorant to the product—so insistently, he reports in his autobiography, that the Zest brand man told the agency he "didn't want to hear another word about deodorant."

But Hobler kept pressing. He told the brand man he'd take the matter to Howard Morgens and Neil McElroy if he had to. Eventually he won his point and Zest became Deodorant Zest, and established itself as a highly successful national brand.

Zest's early advertising was distinctive in two ways. It had a strong (some thought too strong) promise: "For the First Time in Your Life Feel Really Clean"; and it had breakthrough executions in

---

*After Murtfeldt's untimely death, the agency instituted a program of annual physical check-ups for all its officers.

television. It was the first toilet soap to move the action out of the bathroom into wide open watery places: the surf, the sea, rivers, swimming pools. Born in the jingle era, the brand naturally had a jingle, written by Phil Davis. With zestful girls, vivid action and a driving music track, the spots created an exhilarating personality for the brand—"a Zest glow from head to toe," as the jingle put it. The advertising not only made a memorable impact on television audiences—and festival judges; it won several awards and is in the Museum of Modern Art's collection of commercial classics—it started a new trend in the medium. It wasn't long before every beer, cigarette and soft drink had beautiful people cavorting in the surf. Before the Pepsi Generation, there was the Zest Girl* and she was born on B&B's thirteenth floor. (I once had an enviable assignment: Miner Raymond, now associate manager of P&G Productions, and I spent a week in Hollywood, auditioning and filming some fifty what were then called "bathing beauties," looking for the perfect Zest Girl. We never found her.)

   The idea for Gravy Train, the dog food that makes its own gravy, was dreamed up in the kitchen of a former B&B account man, according to Brown Bolté, who later became executive vice-president. Bolté says he developed the idea by dousing dry chunks of dog food with Kitchen Bouquet, baking them, then adding water to produce gravy. He took the idea to General Foods and they took it from there.
   Wherever the original idea came from, it was developed by the technical research department of GF's pet foods division, and introduced by B&B in 1959. From the beginning, Gravy Train had memorable advertising. In print it announced "The World's First Dog Food that Makes its Own Gravy (Right in the Bowl!)," with photography by fashion photographer Irving Penn. Penn also shot the TV commercials with his characteristic high key lighting. Perhaps the most memorable TV spot for Gravy Train happened by accident. Ray Lind, then senior producer on the account, recently described it:
   "We had shot the storyboard and were about to call it a wrap

---

*One Zest Girl was disappointing. When we got her down to Bermuda to film a commercial that called for her to fling herself about in the waves, she confessed she couldn't swim, was afraid of the water. We had to replace her with local talent.

when I saw this little kitten that had been running around the studio. We had a little time left, so I said to John Flagg, 'Let's see what happens when we put the cat with the dog.' So we did, and let the camera roll. John wrote a voice-over commentary to the edited picture, and it turned out so well we never did use the commercial we originally shot.''

"Cat and Dog" won every award in the book, and led to a rash of animal commercials for the brand, including one with baby ducks and a Great Dane.

Distinctive advertising unquestionably helped Gravy Train gain an important share of the market. But the most important factor in its success was an innovative product concept that just may have been born in an agency man's kitchen.

"Please Don't Squeeze the Charmin"

"How do you *demonstrate* softness, not just talk about it?"

That was the question redheaded copy supervisor Jim Haines, redheaded group head Fi Fifield and junior writer John Chervokas were kicking around one day in Chervokas's little office cubicle.

Charmin had been launched in the late '50s with a campaign based on endorsements from such women as the proprietor of a motel and the owner of the Mississippi riverboat *Delta Queen*. There also had been a campaign written by George Panetta starring an animated dog named Gentle.* Both okay, but not exceptional. By the early 1960s Procter & Gamble had developed a new manufacturing process that made a softer product. Now the copy team was pondering how to *show* softness. John Chervokas, now executive vice-president and creative director of Warwick, Welsh & Miller, recalled the historic brainstorming session in an *Advertising Age* article:

> How do you measure something
> like softness?

---

*Panetta, a gentle man himself, was also a novelist and playwright. While writing Charmin copy, his play *King of the Whole Damned World* was playing Off Broadway. He died in 1969 at the age of 59.

Fall on a pillow.
Hug a pillow.
Squeeze a. . . .

What does mom do in the
supermarket? She squeezes
the melons . . . and the tomatoes
to see if they're soft.

Why not use the same test for
Charmin?
Squeeze the Charmin.

Crazy advice? Supermarket
managers will flip their
corks.

Okay then, let's tell them
not to squeeze the Charmin.
Yes. Obsession. Fad. It
becomes the rage to squeeze
the Charmin because it's so
irresistibly soft. . . .

In an hour and a half Chervokas wrote a commercial called
"Digby" that had a supermarket manager named Whipple, named
after George Whipple, then head of B&B PR, saying to women customers, "Squeeze the melons, squeeze the tomatoes, but *please* don't
squeeze the Charmin!"

Vic Bloede recalls the first time he saw the "Digby" commercial: "There was no doubt in my mind that it was a barn burner.
We made a pool, built up the 'Please Don't Squeeze the Charmin'
theme line and took them to Cincinnati. It took some selling, but we
finally got approval."

The commercial was produced by Howard Magwood and
shot, appropriately, in Flushing, New York, with Dick Wilson, Hollywood character actor and former player of acrobatic drunk acts, as
the fussy Mr. Whipple.

When Burke tested it, the recall score went through the ceiling, racking up the highest recall score of any commercial tested up to that time. And sales were equally spectacular. In every market it entered, Charmin became the number one brand.

Eighteen years and some 75 commercials later, the Whipple spots are still moving Charmin off the shelves. Nationally the brand outsells all other toilet tissues.

The fame, and notoriety, of the campaign has spread far and wide. In a newspaper poll in 1978, Mr. Whipple was named the third best-known American just behind former President Nixon and Billy Graham. "Please Don't Squeeze the Charmin" has been emblazoned on T-shirts, greeting cards and is the title of a country western. It has been named by R. H. Bruskin Associates as, far and away, the most recognizable advertising slogan among those tested, being identified by more than eight out of ten persons. If public vilification is a measure of fame, Charmin has garnered plenty of that, too. CROC—the Committee for the Rejection of Obnoxious Commercials—named it among the ten most hated commercials in 1971; and a Toshiba ad in 1978 was headlined: "The Video Cassette Recorder that Lets You Wipe Out Mr. Whipple."

Executive Arabesques

The account supervisor had been fired.

Greatly distraught, and more irascible than ever, he was re-enacting that time-honored corporate ritual of the cashiered executive —packing his files in cardboard boxes.

Ralph, the shoeshine man, on his afternoon rounds, opened the account supervisor's door, stuck his head in and gave a "crick-crack" on his tin cricket. The supervisor, never a kindly man, looked up, saw Ralph and shouted, "Get the hell out of here. I haven't got time for a shine!"

Ralph withdrew his head, closed the door. A moment later he opened it again, stuck his head in and said with the heavy irony only a man who had stared at ad executives' feet all his life could know:

"Big shot!"

Ralph, who shined the Thom McAns, the Bostonians and the Churches at the agency for more than thirty years, had seen many an executive come and go. A stooped, saturnine little man with a wise old monkey's face, he never missed a thing, despite being almost totally deaf. He knew the story behind the account man's departure, knew that he had lost out in a brash, bold play for power.

The account supervisor had steadily undermined the man he reported to, executive vice-president Esty Stowell; had undercut, with distortions and innuendoes, his position with a major client, until Stowell, a proud, pipe-smoking man of patrician elegance, had resigned. In a decision he was rather soon to regret, Lusk promoted the deposer to senior vice-president, even put him on the board of directors. Less than six months later, the deposer himself was deposed, having proved himself inadequate for the new responsibilities given him. Stowell, hurt, retired from advertising to his home in Basking Ridge, New Jersey, for a year or so, finally joined Ogilvy & Mather, and eventually became president. David Ogilvy writes in *Confessions of An Advertising Man*, "It wasn't until Esty Stowell joined up in 1957 . . . that our agency began to acquire a reputation for strength in *all* departments . . . he was a very able man."

The loss of Stowell was deeply regretted by others as well, including Brown Bolté who gives Stowell's departure as one of the reasons for his own resignation, after rising to executive vice-president. (Another reason was his unrequited presidential aspiration. When that goal seemed beyond fulfillment, he resigned and joined Sullivan, Stauffer, Colwell & Bayles, where he served as president for 22 months before leaving to pursue other business interests.)

The leave takings of Stowell and Bolté somewhat depleted the upper executive ranks, leaving Alan Sidnam as the only remaining executive vice-president in account management. To fill one of the gaps, the board elected Bill Hesse executive vice-president, in recognition of his growing responsibility and performance as management supervisor on General Foods.

William Robert Hesse, a stocky, bald, gregarious man, played

professional basketball the first year out of high school before continuing his education, first in architecture, then in pre-law. He finally
settled on psychology and got his master's degree at the University of
Cincinnati. Like Jack Bowen, he began his business career in the sales
department of Procter & Gamble where he brought his sales section
from twenty-second (bottom) position to first place in nine months.
An associate who worked with him at the time said, "He was the only
guy who could bite off more than he could chew—and then chew it."

Les Pearl, well-known copywriter at BBDO in the '40s and
'50s, persuaded Hesse to join that agency after being impressed with
him during their hitch together in the army. "After Bill took a four-
week training course," Pearl recalled, "he knew more about the advertising business than I did after twenty years."

At BBDO Hesse was account supervisor on Lever Brothers,
Crosley and Campbell Soups. He joined Benton & Bowles in 1956 to
work on General Foods. A master salesman of warm presence and
conviction, he also worked on new business presentations.

Sometime after Hesse's elevation to executive vice-president,
Bob Lusk called Alan Sidnam into his office. Sidnam who, before
Hesse's rapid rise had been Lusk's heir apparent, describes the meet-
ing:

"Bob got very emotional. He said he had the highest regard for
me, but that there was another contender for the presidency—Bill
Hesse. I said, 'That's perfectly all right with me. What's the problem?' He said he just wanted me to know. He said, 'I want to give Bill
the chance to go all the way.' Later he offered to make one of us
president and the other chairman. He wanted to cross-ruff us both on
P&G and GF. But I couldn't buy that. I said, 'Don't make me run
in tandem with Bill Hesse.' This was the beginning of a rift between
Bob and me."

When Lusk and the board finally elected Hesse president, Sidnam resigned. Later he joined his old friend, Esty Stowell, at Ogilvy
& Mather as executive vice-president. He now heads his own company, All American Sports.

Two other executive vice-presidents were named in account

management after Sidnam left: Ed Murtfeldt, whose supervisory duties on P&G were expanded, and Ted Steele, the Renaissance Man of the agency who now added responsibility for the international operation to his other duties.

The Tremors of Change

The six-year period 1956–61, saw organizational shifts, not only in account management, but also in the creative department, which was feeling the first tremors of change that eventually would alter agency creative structures throughout the industry.

The first of a series of creative mutations the agency was to experience during the next decade was the consolidation of print and television. With television in 1956 accounting for 57 percent of the billings, management felt it was time to bring the two creative arms together. The intent was for all writers and art directors to work in both media. Actually, there continued to be TV specialists and print specialists for some time, until a new generation of creative people trained in both arts came onto the scene. In the same year Vic Bloede was made copy chief, and two years later he became creative director when Pattison was named vice-chairman and management supervisor on a number of accounts, including Parliament and IBM.

By the late '50s Benton & Bowles's creative reputation, despite a consistently high level of work, was overshadowed by its reputation as a marketing agency. Bob Lusk was not happy about this state of affairs, and was determined to do something about it. He was a chronically discontented man who was always casting an envious eye at the creative work of other agencies and saying, "Why can't *we* do something like that?"

It is not hard to understand why B&B's image was skewed toward marketing, why it was known in the industry as an account-oriented agency. Its dominant figure for 25 years—Atherton Hobler—hadn't built his business career on the Triangle of Marketing Success for nothing. Hobler, first and foremost, was a *marketing* man, one of the most knowledgeable and skillful of his time. He was not an especially gifted creative man, although while he occupied the seat of power he acted like one, and strongly influenced the creative direction of the agency.*

What was needed to improve the creative image, Lusk believed, was someone new from the outside, a strong personality with a proven record as a creative superstar, someone who could come in and change things overnight. Lusk had a weakness for the charismatic outsider, a belief in the mysterious stranger who would turn up one day with his silver bullet and put everything right. He became infatuated, and later disenchanted, with many such persons during his career.**

The man chosen to put new luster on B&B's creative reputation was Bill Tyler, whom Hobler had met while playing golf in Florida. He joined the agency in 1958 as senior vice-president in charge of creative services, with Bloede continuing as creative director. The following year Tyler was elected executive vice-president.

Tyler had been copy chief and chairman of the plans board at Leo Burnett in Chicago, and had a reputation, reinforced by his monthly "Top Ten" column in *Advertising Age*, as one of the industry's most astute judges of advertising—"tough and pointed as a blade," as one writer called him. A former tennis pro with a lean, trim figure and close-cropped mustache (his Burnett colleague Draper Daniels once titled a profile of him "Vinegar Jug with a Mustache"), Tyler had a sharp, acerbic mind and caustic wit that cut through cant like a hot knife through butter. Commenting on a "pompous poop" —a favorite phrase of his—he once said, "He's very articulate— *mouths every single word!*"

To add new muscle to the department, Tyler and Bloede brought in a clutch of creative heavyweights: Bob Pliskin as head of the art department; and Al Goldman, Jean Brown, Leo Higdon and Bernie Lubar as creative supervisors.

---

*A clue to the agency's fundamental attitude toward creativity's place in the sceme of things can be found in a new business presentation prepared in September 1959. It lists what it calls Five Basic B&B Philosophies. The first four deal with marketing and account management. The fifth and last mentions creativity.

**In retrospect, the level of creative work the agency was turning out during this period of critical self-appraisal was generally high, often exceptional. The problem was not so much the agency's creative product as it was—and this was Lusk's concern—how the outside world *perceived* B&B, and that was primarily as a marketing agency.

A man passionately devoted to words, the *exactly* right words, Tyler's chief interest and experience was in print. Shortly after his arrival at B&B he boiled down his creative credo to a single sentence: "One Strong, Simple Selling Idea Dramatically Presented." Though not as simple as Ted Bates's USP (Unique Selling Proposition), it was more inclusive and was the agency's first creative rallying cry.

Tyler's silver bullet was the CRC—Creative Review Committee (an import from Burnett)—which consisted of himself and Bloede, and a rotating group of other top creative people. Meeting two or three times a week, the CRC's purpose was to pass on advertising before its presentation to the account group and client. For most creative people CRC meetings were mildly abrasive sessions in which their darlings were sometimes maimed or murdered by Tyler, but often were strengthened and improved. For others, especially women copywriters, they were a season in hell from which they often emerged in tears. Tyler sometimes seemed to come down especially hard on women members of the department. Commenting on a woman copywriter, he once said, "She may be all right, but I'd hate to be standing in her way at 5 o'clock when she's headed for the elevator."

The copywriters and art directors weren't the only ones who chafed under the Tyler regime. Vic Bloede, finding the relationship with Tyler increasingly awkward and unsatisfactory, decided to leave. When word got out that he was unhappy, he had two offers, one from Norman Strouse, president of J. Walter Thompson, the other from David Ogilvy. One Friday afternoon, still mulling over which offer to take, Bloede went up to the seventeenth floor to tell Lusk he was resigning, but Lusk had left for the day. He went to Hesse's office, but he wasn't in, either. He ended up in Alan Sidnam's office. Sidnam recounts what happened: "We had a long talk, then we went out to dinner. I told Vic it would be a mistake to quit. I told him to bide his time, that things would change, that he had strengths that went beyond creative. I said, 'With your background and talents, you could be president of this agency some day.' He said, 'You must be kidding.' But he decided to stay."

The Crew Carries On

As so often happens, the *sturm und drang* that shakes the upper structure of an organization was barely felt by the people who did the day-to-day work. While the officers on the bridge pondered what course to take, the crew members below deck were quietly doing the same top grade professional job they always had done.

In research, headed in 1958 by Dick Casey, the emphasis began to shift more and more from marketing to the test of the agency's own product, its creative work. Dr. Art Wilkins set up an advertising research unit, and was one of the first in the industry to experiment with measurement of *persuasive* values of commercials. Today, at least 90 percent of research's activity is focused on advertising, as opposed to product and market-testing.

Before he moved into account management, Pattison experimented with his own brand of advertising research. Casey recalls Pattison's project:

"Pat believed the research methods then used failed to measure the emotional response to advertising; he was tired of those low recall scores he was getting. So he went to Al Whittaker (then head of research)* and asked him to come up with a way to test how people *felt* about advertising. 'You don't want research,' Al said. 'You want promotion.' He gave him Pete Nicholas, and Pat and Pete developed what they called EQ—Emotional Quotient. Pat was very secretive about how it worked. He had a big presentation before 300 B&Bers at the Barbizon Plaza with live music and a slide show. But it was short-lived. Neither P&G nor our own research department would endorse it."

In 1959 B&B became the first agency to consolidate media and programming in a single media management organization. Lee Rich became the first director of the new department, with Ollie Barbour

---

*Whittaker later became president of Bristol Myers, and executive vice-president of the Mennen Company. He is now executive director of the Institute for International Development.

as director of programming (later replaced by Grant Tinker*), Hal Miller as manager of media and Lee Curlin media director. The record of programming successes begun by Tom McDermott was continued under Rich. In the 1962–63 season the agency had six out of the ten top TV shows (*Red Skelton, Ben Casey, Danny Thomas, Andy Griffith, Dick Van Dyke* and *Gunsmoke*), three of them produced by B&B. In the aggregate they represented an advertising-entertainment investment of more than $28 million.

In the creative department, the writers, art directors and producers, largely oblivious to the creative arabesques, were turning out distinctive campaigns such as these:

"Cup-and-a-Half of Flavor" for Instant Maxwell House Coffee. Conceived by Art Kramer and Dick Ende, the campaign had one of television's more arresting visuals: As a cup of coffee was poured, the coffee miraculously rose an inch or so above the rim of the cup. Produced by Si Merrill, probably the agency's most knowledgeable film technician, the special effect took six months and $150,000 to bring off.

"Aged Coffee Beans" for Yuban. An audacious, innovative idea in coffee advertising, created by Howard Shank (later president of Leo Burnett, Inc.).

"Skip It," for Western Union. A highly visible, award-winning print campaign that got record Starch readership ratings.

"The New York Woman: When Her Needs are Financial Her Reaction is Chemical" for Chemical Bank of New York. A breakthrough campaign originated by copy supervisor Gene Schinto (later a creative director at Grey Advertising), it was the first bank advertising to direct its message to women. The commercials were among the first to have the fast closeup action and crisp editing that characterized the "New York School" of commercial film-making. They also had exciting music tracks conceived and produced by music director

---

*Tinker, married to Mary Tyler Moore, is now head of MTM Productions. Other B&B media/programming people who've moved to other jobs in the industry include: Lew Wechsler, program head of Wells Rich Greene; Irwin Siegelstein, NBC executive vice-president; Lee Curlin, NBC program executive, Phil Capice, independent producer for Lorimar Productions; Dick Gershon, principal of Lois Pitts Gershon; Merrill Grant, media/programming head of Case McGrath; Hal Miller, media/programming head of Sullivan, Stauffer, Colwell & Bayles; Alan Wagner, CBS program executive.

Roy Eaton. Eaton, a talented concert pianist and former child prodigy, began his career as a copywriter and jingle writer at Y&R. He was hired by Bloede in 1959, the first black in advertising to be elected a vice-president and head a department.

"A Little Bit Better," for Post Cereals,* Pat Pattison's idea, with a jingle and a hand sign created by producer Lou Hanousek. (Air India is currently—1979—using the same line.)

"Never Carry More Cash than You Can Afford to Lose," for American Express. This durable campaign line first appeared in 1957, and featured testimonials by stars such as Patrice Munsel, Ida Lupino, Robert Taylor, Dick Powell, George Burns and Gracie Allen.**

In the spring of 1961 B&B won nine Clio Awards given by the American TV Commercials Festival, the highest number ever awarded a single agency.

"Tide's In . . . Tide's Out!"

"We waited a long time for the other shoe to drop."

A former agency account man was talking. "We knew it was coming," he said, "but when it finally did, it was still a hell of a shock."

The loss of the $10 million Tide account in December 1961 was the most traumatic experience in the agency's history next to the loss of Colgate twenty years earlier.

The loss was particularly painful for Hobler and Lusk, who had seen the brand grow from a test market product with modest expectations, to the nation's number one laundry product. The loss of

---

*For ten years or so during the '60s and '70s, the chief copywriter on Post cereals was Frank Corre. Virtually a one-man creative department, he created animated characters, staged the action, wrote his own music and lyrics. The last holdout against the art/copy team system, he worked alone, using an art director, Mort Leav, mainly as a storyboard artist. Corre died of a heart attack in 1978. He was 45.

**Other celebrities featured in agency-produced advertising include: Lou Gehrig (Huskies); Jack Benny, Bob Hope, Ethel Merman (Texaco); Euell Gibbons (Post Grape Nuts); George Montgomery (Pledge); Amy Vanderbilt (Glade); Florence Henderson (Jubilee); Van Johnson (Grape Nuts Flakes); Jerry Lewis (Hasbro Toys); J. Paul Getty (E.F. Hutton); Yogi Berra (NP 27); Rocky Graziano (Post Raisin Bran); Bill Cosby (Crest); John Wayne, Buddy Hackett, Dr. Michael E. De-Bakey (American Cancer Society); Ezzard Charles (Muscular Dystrophy Association).

billings was bad enough; what hurt even more was the thought that the agency had lost P&G's confidence.*

Tide's troubles began at least two years before its departure. After getting the jump on the market in the late '40s and dominating it for several years, competition moved in with a proliferation of product improvements and additives. Lever Brothers launched No-Rinse Surf during a serious water shortage. Colgate's Fab and P&G's own Cheer offered products with bleach, whiteners, brighteners and water softeners. Low- and medium-sudsers flooded the market. Tide, a high-sudser with no recent product improvements it could talk about in its advertising, continued to decline gradually in market share. Lacking product superiority, Tide's only hope of stemming the decline, the agency felt, was an exciting creative idea, an idea that would lift the brand out of the "hoh-hum" laundry product category.

When copywriters Joan Lipton and Nort Wolf came up with "Cleanest Clean Under the Sun" everybody—client and agency alike —thought this might be the breakthrough idea. A first commercial got a fair Burke score,** but the playback of copy points was poor. Client and agency agreed to produce another pool of commercials that, they hoped, would correct this weakness. Despite commercials that were visually beautiful, and even won a place in the permanent collection of the Museum of Modern Art, the "Cleanest Clean" campaign did not break the bank in research scores and was abandoned.

Now it was back to the drawing board with a growing sense of forboding. Virtually everybody in the creative department was enlisted in the big push. Commercial after commercial, produced by big Ed Anderson and his assistant Manning Rubin, were shot and tested. Testimonial commercials were tried. Animation commercials

---

*The departure of Tide, though a bitter experience, did not affect the agency's relationship with Procter & Gamble, which continued to assign it new products at regular intervals. Pampers had been assigned in 1961. Others followed: Scope mouthwash (1963); Bonus detergent (1965); Dawn dishwashing liquid and Bounce fabric softener (1970); Rely (1973); Wondra (1976).

**Reduced to its essentials, the Burke system of measuring the effectiveness of television commercials works like this: A commercial is run on, usually, two or more stations. The next day an interviewer telephones a sampling of viewers. After determining that the person has seen the show in which the commercial appeared, the interviewer asks if they saw the commercial, and if so, what they remember about it. The score—say a 30—means that 30 percent of the people who were watching the program in which the test commercial appeared, remembered seeing it and can describe what they saw.

Robert E. Lusk followed Colgate to Ted Bates in 1941, then returned to B&B in 1944. He was president from 1954 to 1961, and chairman of the board from 1962 to 1967. He died in 1971, a victim of Lou Gehrig's disease.

Ted Steele, during a 37-year career, held jobs in research, programming and media, account management, and international, with an array of titles that included senior vice-president, executive vice-president, chairman of the board and chairman of the executive committee. He retired in 1973.

First campaign for Tide, the "washday miracle" that launched the detergent decade.

H.O. (Pat) Pattison, Jr.,
creative director during the
'40s and '50s before mov-
ing to account man-
agement. He retired as
chairman of the executive
committee in 1965.

Vic Bloede (in foreground)
and John Gubelman,
copywriter, in the early
'50s, when Bloede was copy
group head on American
Association of Railroads.
They are getting the feel of
the account by riding the
caboose of a freight train
from New York to Chicago.

B&B's College of Advertising Knowledge, post-W.W. II program for indoctrinating returning veterans. From left, standing: Jean Finegan, Bob Kane, [unidentified], Charlie Fisher, Dave Burt. Seated: Clarence Goshorn and Quent McDonald, who ran the program.

An early (1950–51) animated spot for Post Sugar Crisp featuring Super Crisp Bears and jingle by music director Len McKenzie ("As a cereal it's dandy, for snacks it's so handy, or eat it like candy!")

First filmed commercial produced for Maxwell House Coffee (1949) recreated the historic moment when Teddy Roosevelt sipped the brew and uttered for the first time the immortal phrase, "Good to the last drop!"

Actress Tallulah Bankhead sued Procter & Gamble and B&B for $500,000 when McKenzie's jingle, "Tallulah the Tube of Prell," hit the air in the early '50s. Agency legal counsel Gil Gilbert settled the suit for $7,000 after a barrelful of free publicity for both Bankhead and the brand, including a two-page spread in Life magazine.

Billboard featuring CONOCO slogan, created by the agency in the mid-'50s, which the oil company is still using.

RUCKER-HILBERT
9401

BENTON & BOWLES, INC.
STOCKHOLDERS MEETING
THE WALDORF-ASTORIA   NEW YORK CITY
APRIL 18, 1949

B&B family portrait at a 1949 stockholders' meeting at the Waldorf-Astoria Hotel. In pictures of earlier annual meetings, copywriter Lee Beulow used to routinely stick out her tongue as the camera shutter clicked.

Ed Murtfeldt, the man Jack Bowen said "typified the B&B character at its best." Elected executive vice-president in 1961, he could have been president, but didn't "want to be out in front that much." He died at age 56, while playing paddle tennis.

Alan Sidnam was account supervisor on Tide, sharing the brand's meteoric rise. He became executive vice-president in 1957, resigned in 1961. Later he held a similar post at Ogilvy & Mather.

AMAZING COFFEE DISCOVERY!

Not a powder! Not a grind! But millions of tiny "FLAVOR BUDS" of <u>real</u> coffee . . . ready to burst instantly into that famous MAXWELL HOUSE FLAVOR!

Utterly unlike old-style "instants" . . . just as quick but tastes so different!

In the famous Maxwell House kitchens this superb, roaster-fresh coffee is actually brewed for you. At the exact moment of perfection the water is removed by a special Maxwell House process—leaving the millions of miracle "Flavor Buds"!

100% Pure Coffee—No Fillers Added!

Just add hot water . . . and the bursting "Flavor Buds" flood your cup with coffee as delicious as the best you've ever brewed. One sip and you'll never go back to old ways!

Saves you money, too! The large economy-size jar saves up to 75¢, compared to three pounds of ground coffee!

See how the Flavor Buds "come to life" in your cup!

MAGNIFIED VIEW of new miracle "Flavor Buds" shows how utterly different they are from old-style powders and grinds.

THE INSTANT you add hot water, the "Flavor Buds" burst—releasing flood of rich, delicious Maxwell House flavor!

Reach for the jar with the stars on top!

A Product of General Foods

The only instant coffee with that GOOD-TO-THE-LAST-DROP flavor!

Introductory ad for Instant Maxwell House, which ran unchanged for seven years.

Tom McDermott, director of programming in the early '50s, the agency's youngest vice-president at 22.

Lee Rich, first director of media management, after media and program departments were consolidated in 1959.

Brown Bolté, account supervisor on P&G brands during the '40s and '50s. He resigned in 1958 as executive vice-president to become, briefly, president of Sullivan, Stauffer, Colwell & Bayles.

Gordon Webber in the early '50s when he was assistant head of television department.

Ray Lind (left) head of TV art department in 1951, and Wes Emmart, TV art director, with prop for Captain Video, *early TV series produced by B&B.*

Cast of Mama, *top-rated TV series from 1949–57, sponsored by Maxwell House Coffee. From left: Dick Van Patten as Nels; Judson Laire, Papa; Robin Morgan, Dagmar; Rosemary Rice, Katrin; Peggy Wood, Mama.*

Now — 1956 — Procter & Gamble proudly announces . . .

TRIUMPH
OVER
TOOTH DECAY

Crest Toothpaste with Fluoristan
strengthens tooth enamel to lock out decay from within

Fluoristan is Procter & Gamble's exclusive <u>stannous</u> fluoride formula—proven the greatest decay-preventive in any toothpaste

Miracle of the Towns Without Toothaches. For years, children in certain towns were virtually without cavities. Nature's decay-preventive, *fluoride*, was in their drinking water!

Science Long Tried to Capture Fluoride in a toothpaste. At last, university scientists discovered *Fluoristan* — the greatest decay-preventive in any toothpaste.

Fluoristan Makes Possible Crest. Without Fluoristan, you cannot get maximum protection against tooth decay with a toothpaste. Protects teeth of adults and children, six and over.

Dentists Tested Crest for three year on 5,673 people. No toothpaste ca end all decay, but Crest set records decay prevention *never approached P any other toothpaste.*

IMPORTANT

Crest with Fluoristan is the only toothpaste ever developed that makes possible a major reduction in tooth decay for everyone, everywhere, by strengthening tooth enamel. Thereby, Crest marks a turning point in man's age-old struggle against this almost universal disease.

Instead of waiting helplessly for cavities to strike, Crest now makes it possible for you to build strong defenses against decay *within teeth* ... to *fortify* teeth so that they turn back the destructive attacks of decay (as opposed to the old-fashioned method of brushing a temporary coating of protection on the surface of teeth). With Crest, your family approaches the long dreamed-of day of healthy, decay-free teeth.

NO OTHER TOOTHPASTE PREVENTS DECAY LIKE CREST

©1956, The Procter & Gamble C

Introductory ad for Crest with Fluoristan, stannous fluoride formula developed by P&G and scientists at University of Indiana. Brand became leader after ADA endorsement in 1960.

Jack Bowen at about the time he joined the agency in 1959, as a member of Bob Wallace's marketing department. After a year as account executive on Prell, he became account supervisor on Crest, helping move the brand to Number One position.

Dick Casey, director of research from 1959 to 1964, when he moved to senior vice-president for administration. He retired in 1978.

"Look, Mom—No Cavities!" campaign, launched in late '50s, became one of advertising's most memorable slogans.

Atherton Hobler with prize-winning Guernsey at his farm outside Princeton, New Jersey in 1962. From left: Philip Lampel, New Jersey Secretary of Agriculture, Hobler, R.D. Stewart, executive secretary of the American Guernsey Cattle Club. Hobler's herds set milk-producing records that still stand.

An early Zest ad (1952). Zest TV spots were first to move action from bathroom to outdoor scenes.

Esty Stowell rose from the mailroom to executive vice-president in charge of General Foods accounts. He resigned in 1957, later became president of Ogilvy & Mather.

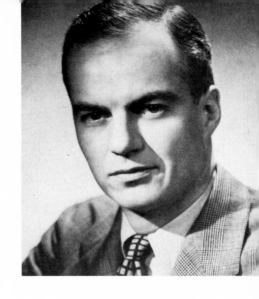

Agency had Philip Morris account from 1951 to 1966 . . .

. . . and American Express Travelers Cheques from 1949 to 1962. Bob Hope turned up years later as a spokesman for Texaco.

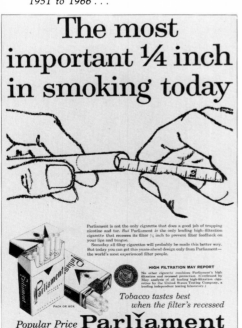

The most important ¼ inch in smoking today

Parliament is not the only cigarette that does a good job of trapping nicotine and tar. But Parliament *is* the only leading high-filtration cigarette that recesses its filter ¼ inch to prevent filter feedback on your lips and tongue.

Someday all filter cigarettes will probably be made this better way. But today you can get this years-ahead design only from Parliament—the world's most experienced filter people.

HIGH FILTRATION MAY REPORT
No other cigarette combines Parliament's high filtration and recessed protection. (Confirmed by May analysis of all leading high-filtration cigarettes by the United States Testing Company, a leading independent testing laboratory.)

Tobacco tastes best when the filter's recessed

Popular Price **Parliament**

PACK OR BOX

"*I never carry more than* $50 *in cash,*"

says **BOB HOPE** star of "PARIS HOLIDAY" in Technirama Technicolor, a United Artists' Release

"*When I travel, I always carry my money in American Express Travelers Cheques.* Spendable anywhere, good until used, prompt refund if lost or stolen. Buy them at your BANK, at Railway Express and Western Union offices. Charges, only a penny a dollar."

AMERICAN EXPRESS

AMERICAN EXPRESS TRAVELERS CHEQUES

NEVER CARRY MORE CASH THAN YOU CAN AFFORD TO LOSE

were tried. A Hollywood show writer knocked out a couple of scripts. Even Hobler, now in his seventies, pitched in like a man whose house was on fire, and wrote a commercial—one from the old Stand-Up-And-By-God-Tell-'Em school of the late '40s.

But nothing worked. Research scores continued to disappoint.

Black Christmas

One week before Christmas—a hard-luck season in a hard-luck year (a few months earlier, Bob Ellis, young assistant producer, was killed in an air crash while delivering a Tide test commercial to Cincinnati)—the other shoe finally dropped. Procter & Gamble informed the agency that they were transferring the Tide account to Compton.

In anticipation of the sharp drop in income, a sizable number of people were dismissed. The gloom was profound.

Leaving at the end of the day for the long Christmas weekend, a number of us were talking about the heads that were rolling, wondering who'd be next, while we waited for the elevator. In the group was Dave McEneny, copywriter on Johnson and department wit. The elevator arrived and McEneny got on, saying to the rest of us with a wave, "Well, Merry Christmas, every other one of you"*

A sense, almost, of relief settled on the agency after the departure of Tide. The struggle with an intractable problem against mounting odds was over, and now everybody could move on to other problems and challenges.

There would be plenty of both in the decade ahead.

---

*McEneny is the originator of another elevator remark that has entered the folklore of business. Squeezed into the front of a crowded elevator facing the wrong way, Dave rode in silence for a moment, then said to the people facing him, "I suppose you wonder why I called you all together."

Seven

The Stressful '60s
1962–67

"*I*f you want somebody to do storyboards for you, get yourself a trained ape!"

Art director Dick Ende was mad. He was fed up with dutifully drawing pictures, illustrating copywriters' commercials without being consulted about them beforehand. When a copy supervisor gave him one more commercial to storyboard, he stormed in to see Vic Bloede.

After listening with a sympathetic ear to Ende's complaint, Bloede agreed that maybe the system needed changing. The blowup marked the beginning of the copy/art team concept in the agency's creative department. Before that, copywriters wrote their commercials off by themselves and gave them to an art director, or "storyboard artist" as they were then called, who drew the scenes the writer had described under "Video Instructions." After the Ende revolt, ADs started to work with writers before anything was put down on paper, and began to assume a new status in the creative hierarchy.

Ende's small revolution was merely a hint of the ferment that had begun to unsettle and alter the creative structures of advertising agencies throughout the industry. In between the Silent '50s and the Have-A-Nice-Day '70s, was the Stressful '60s—the decade of dissent. Fueled by Vietnam, civil rights battles and general social unrest, it had spawned a generation of rebels, with and without causes. Many of them either dropped out of, or never joined, the Establishment.* Others, if they joined it, did so more or less on their own terms. An article in *Television/Radio Age* described this "new young breed of creative revolutionary" in advertising:

---

*Personnel director Gil Walker recalls the problem the agency had recruiting young people for account management work during the '60s. "We had a hard time finding good people who wanted to come into advertising. Everybody was turned off a business career. Even economics majors verbally attacked us as representatives of Big Business."

(They are) lately of Princeton, Pratt, City College, Erasmus Hall and the Woodstock Festival. A lot of them are war babies. Hip, cool, loose and aware. In short, the Alienated Generation, in headlong revolt against their fathers, their fathers' money, Lawrence Welk, Spiro Agnew, air pollution and the Vietnam war. They are also, to the considerable enrichment—and sometimes pain—of our industry, in passionate revolt against dull, ordinary advertising.

At Benton & Bowles, as with most agencies, the "new creatives" had a profound impact, not only on the advertising, but on the life style of the agency. With the newly liberated art director in the vanguard, they moved into the plain offices of 666 Fifth Avenue with their art posters, mobiles and pop artifacts, and set the place on its ear.

One woman art director's office was decorated exclusively with batik pillows and incense—no furniture; she drew her layouts lying on her stomach on the floor. Another art director, a man, painted a *trompe l'oeil* picture on the wall of his inside cubicle—a view out of a window into a window of a hotel room showing a naked couple in bed. John Cross, a copywriter, installed a barber's chair in his office ("I can think better stretched out in it," he said), and for a time came to work in white overalls and a house painter's cap with "Moore's Paints" printed on it. Almost everybody, of course, wore blue jeans, the raggeder the better—except some women who wore Mother Hubbards. "B&B" now meant "beards and beads"—the standard accouterments of male members of the department. One writer who commuted from some conservative Westchester enclave used to arrive at the office in Brooks Brothers suit, shirt and tie, then change into his hippie uniform—torn jeans and worn sneakers—so he would be *au courant* with his colleagues. Another blue-jeaned writer kept a proper suit in his office for client calls.

The contrast between the laid-back dress style of the creative people and the rest of the agency was never more evident than one day in a confrontation between executive vice-president Ted Steele and copywriter Ed Hannibal.* Hannibal, in obligatory blue jeans and

---

*Hannibal, another ad man/novelist, has published four works of fiction, now is a creative group head at William Esty.

faded denim shirt, was waiting for an UP elevator. A DOWN elevator opened to reveal Steele, impeccable in double-breasted pinstripe, custom-made shirt and tie, carrying his Vuitton attaché case. Hannibal, in a wild mood of mock envy, cried out, "Ah, someday I, too, shall be as elegantly turned out as Ted Steele!"

Steele, running a disdainful eye over Hannibal's scruffy jeans and long hair, said, just as the elevator door closed, "Apply yourself, my boy, apply yourself."

But with all the quick changes in dress and identity, the new wave of creative people was making its ideas and inventions felt on the advertising it produced. Most commercials by now were on film, with only 5 to 10 percent on videotape, and film became the passion, the religion of the new generation. For most of the '60s the agency had a weekly film program (Theatre 13, on the thirteenth floor) which showed animation shorts, experimental, avant-garde and foreign footage aimed at expanding the film knowledge of the creative staff. Actually, the screenings attracted as many young account executives, who were beginning to let their hair grow, as creative people. There was also a TV workshop which produced, over a four-year period, some fifteen experimental commercials, at least half of which became prototypes of new campaigns.

The creative ferment in the agencies had its counterpart in the film industry. Along with the new breed of agency creative persons, a new kind of film director began to appear. Many of them were former still photographers such as Mike Eliot, Peter Elgar, Fred Levinson, Bob Bean, Bert Stern, Harold Becker, Steve Horn and Irving Penn. Others, including Marshall Stone, Phil Landeck, Bruce Malmuth, George Gage, Lear Levin and Lenny Hershfield started as "gofers" or apprentices in the emerging "New York School" of film, which owed nothing to the Hollywood big-picture tradition. Responsive to the needs of the closeup medium, the new artisans applied newly developed techniques, notably the hand-held camera, to the requirements of advertising. The result was a new look—a "New York Look"—in television commercials, a synthesis of intimate, fluid movement and dynamic editing that eventually would find its way into feature film-making.

The creative revolution's most far-reaching effect probably

was the "boutique" agency. Almost every old line agency, and some new line ones as well, became the "rejected parent" of one or more such agencies, small spinoff shops which, typically, offered primarily creative services. Not all of these experiments survived to become a Wells Rich Greene (a spinoff of Jack Tinker & Partners), or a Della Femina, Travisano & Partners (Jerry Della Femina, author of *From Those Wonderful Folks Who Gave You Pearl Harbor** was previously with Ted Bates). Most of the boutiques had, and still have, a short life. But several have established themselves firmly, including at least eight whose principals peeled off from B&B.**

The Cost of Revolution

Revolutions cost money, and the creative revolution was no exception. In the production area, the cost of television commercials began to climb about the time the art director became a strong influence in the creative process.*** Understandably more interested in esthetics than accounting, ADs sometimes dreamed up concepts that sent production budgets soaring like the Red Balloon. Extravaganzas such as Contac's "Broadway Lights" and United Airlines' "Dancers" cost more than $100,000, and some of the more exotically-staged automobile commercials were price-tagged at $250,000 and more. Average costs shot up 72 percent during the five-year period 1963–67, according to a 4As study prepared by Manning Rubin, senior vice-president and creative director at Grey and a former B&B producer.

Clients, feeling the pain of rising costs and mystified about why commercials had to cost so much, began to ask hard questions of their agencies. Ray Lind remembers one client's reaction to the problem. "Philip Morris decided to find out exactly what in hell made the cost of commercials so high. So they sent their accountant along on a

---

*Della Femina's spoof headline for the Japanese electronics manufacturer, Panasonic.

**Case & McGrath (Pat McGrath was an account executive); Scali, McCabe & Sloves, now affiliated with Ogilvy & Mather (Ed McCabe was a copywriter); Lord, Geller, Federico, Einstein (Dick Lord was a creative supervisor, Gene Federico an art director and Arthur Einstein a copywriter); Nadler & Larimer (both Arch Nadler and Bob Larimer were copywriters); Lois, Pitts, Gershon (Dick Gershon was manager of the media department); Epstein, Raboy (Mitch Epstein was a co-creative director); Catalano & Gornick (Vito Catalano was an art director); Griffin Bacal (Tom Griffin was a management supervisor, Joe Bacal an associate creative director).

***There were other reasons for high production costs: the advent of color (which overnight added 25 percent); more sophisticated formats; use of "star" directors (Howard Zieff's standard rate was $10,000 a day); and greater use of custom music.

Parliament shoot at Cypress Gardens. They found out one reason, at least: the crew sat down there in forty-degree temperature for ten days waiting for the sun to shine."

By the mid-'60s, the agency was buying more than $6 million worth of commercial production services a year. To bring this sizable volume of spending under management control, it set up a central cost-estimating section under Jim Carroll,* the first operation of its kind in advertising. It also developed, in cooperation with Procter & Gamble and General Foods, other cost control procedures. In 1970 P&G entered into a two-year production consolidation plan with MPO, then the major producer of television commercials. Out of this plan, developed and supervised by P&G Productions associate manager Miner Raymond, emerged a system of buying based on cost plus fixed fee, which eventually was adopted by all ten Procter & Gamble agencies, as well as all B&B clients. Marjorie Kalens, who worked with Raymond in developing the plan, became the agency's production-cost estimator for P&G brands after the consolidation arrangement with MPO was discontinued. In 1977 she was named vice-president and manager of financial production control.

Corporate Consciousness-Raising

Another manifestation of the unrest of the '60s, the civil rights movement, had its impact on the advertising industry as it did on every other segment of the business community. In 1966 a group of militant blacks picketed Benton & Bowles demanding, among other things, that it hire more minority-group members. Although B&B was, in the words of Mrs. Flo Kennedy, the attorney who organized the picketing, "a liberal agency," it had been singled out as a target for the militant group's campaign against the entire advertising agency. A series of meetings followed between president Bill Hesse, Gil Walker, the Urban Coalition and other civil rights groups, and eventually a program of voluntary affirmative action was developed. Two years after the consciousness-raising confrontation with the rights

---

*Carroll, who had been an estimator at Audio Productions, later became manager of the production department. He is now vice-president and manager of broadcast production at Kenyon & Eckhart.

groups, the agency could report that 10.9 percent of its employees were non-white, the best record at the time of any agency.

"I give Bill Hesse, who served on the Urban Coalition board, a lot of the credit for this effort," Dick Casey, then senior vice-president for administration, said recently. "He set the direction and insisted that department heads follow open hiring policies, and that employees must be judged solely on the basis of performance where raises and promotions were concerned." The affirmative action program was shortly after expanded to include women.

"Today [1979]," says Walker, "14.2 percent of the agency's employees are members of minority groups, and 59 percent are women. Of employees at professional (nonsecretarial) levels, 55 percent are women." (In the late '40s the only woman account executive the agency had was Chet Bowles's former secretary, Bonnie Cox, who worked on the Walter Baker's Chocolate account. In 1979 the agency had forty women in account management.)

It seems hard today to imagine it, but as late as 1965 it was a rare thing to see a black face in a television commercial. In the general soul-searching going on during that period, the commercial production committee of the 4As of which I was chairman, decided to do something about it. In a series of seminars for agencies held in New York, Chicago and Los Angeles in 1967, we demonstrated ways non-white talent could be integrated naturally and relevantly into television advertising. With the active cooperation of several major clients, including General Foods and Procter & Gamble, minority-group talent began to turn up in television spots. From an occasional curiosity, the appearance of nonwhites in commercials steadily increased, until today it is commonplace.*

In another voluntary effort, the agency produced for the New York State Human Rights Commission a series of commercials with the theme, "How Would You Feel?" Under the supervision of music director Roy Eaton who also wrote the music tracks, the spots dramatized the damaging psychological effects of discrimination.

---

*When racial integration of commercials first began, one client tested audience reaction to them. The tests showed two things: there was virtually no critical reaction, and commercials with blacks scored moderately, but consistently, higher than commercials with all-white casts, probably because of their novelty.

In programming, Bill Cosby in 1965 became the first black to play a leading role in a television series—*I Spy.* Soon after, black performers began assuming roles in such shows as *Mission Impossible, Hogan's Heroes, Mod Squad* and *Hawaii Five-O.*

Change Titles and Dance

Bill Hesse's move to president in 1962 set in motion a number of other changes in the executive suite, and one high level resignation.

Bob Lusk, still chief executive officer, became chairman of the board. Atherton Hobler, now 72 but still very close to the business, assumed a new title created especially for him by his old friend and legal counsel to the agency, Gil Gilbert—founder chairman. Though technically not accurate, it seemed appropriate. Pat Pattison, who had been vice-chairman, inherited Hobler's title of chairman of the executive committee. For some reason, executive vice-president Bill Tyler wasn't told beforehand about Pattison's promotion. When he learned about it, he submitted his resignation, and somewhat to his surprise, it was accepted. Vic Bloede then was named senior vice-president in charge of creative services, and Al Goldman was appointed copy chief.

Alfred L. Goldman, a solidly built man with gray crewcut, glasses and a rugged, intelligent face, looks like a prizefighter who has retired before anyone ever laid a serious glove on him. In fact, he grew up in the fight world—New Orleans—where his father was a sports writer for the *Item,* and manager of such ring luminaries as Pete Herman, world bantamweight champion, and light heavyweight champion Tony Canzoneri. He began his advertising career in 1949 as a writer with Van Sant Dugdale, Baltimore. Before joining B&B in 1959, he was copy director of Reach-McClinton. A thoroughgoing professional trained in the pragmatic school of drug advertising, Goldman was a critic of advertising, and especially television advertising that was, as he once wrote in a newspaper guest column, "dedicated exclusively to entertaining the customer." A sound strategist, he applied his analytical judgment to the agency's creative product at a time when it needed it most—during the creative revolution when all too often the medium was the message, and form dominated content. Throughout advertising's love affair with filmic fireworks and award-winning commercials that didn't sell—which he called "sheer creative delinquency"—Goldman insisted that it was okay for advertising to be "bright, winsome and charming . . . but not by paying the penalty of failing to talk to the product's bread-and-butter market, or by blurring and wiping out a sharp, clean and powerful selling stance."

More Reorganization

On April 19, 1963, advertising news columnist Jack O'Dwyer wrote in the New York *Journal-American:* "The problem of 'coping with the tremendous amount of information available within today's agency and channeling it to the proper uses' came to the fore today as Benton & Bowles announced a major reorganization of its operations into five 'areas of management.' "

The new organizational concept recognized, as a presentation prepared for Beech-Nut Life Savers stated, that "the raw material of our activity—the life stuff of which our advertising is made—is *information*—(which) . . . is perishable. As information about people, products and markets, it is subject to obsolescence—and requires continuous updating and replenishment."

The five areas of management, each under the supervision of a board member, were: information, creative, media, account and administrative. The reorganization was the lynch pin of the agency's new management strategy that attempted to come to grips with the growing complexities of a rapidly growing business.

In 1963, in a move toward fulfillment of the prophecy made by Alan Sidnam three years before, Vic Bloede was named executive vice-president and management supervisor on Procter & Gamble. To replace Bloede as creative head, Bill Hesse believed he had just the man: his longtime friend and colleague at BBDO—Whit Hobbs.

Hobbs, who had been copy chief at BBDO, came to Benton & Bowles in May 1963 as senior vice-president in charge of creative services. At the same time, Al Goldman was made senior vice-president and creative director. A tall, tennis-playing Connecticut Yankee with a country drawl that belies his Harvard background, Hobbs had made a considerable reputation in the industry as a speaker before advertising and marketing groups. A witty, satiric critic of dull and strident advertising that takes itself too seriously, he urged his audiences, and his creative colleagues at B&B, to "sell unto others as you'd have them sell unto you, with friendship and gentle persuasion. Keep your aim high, and your voice low."

A frequent silent straight woman in Hobbs's speeches was—and is—his wife Kit who, he says, is so compulsively neat that she gets up early and cleans the house on the day the cleaning woman is coming.

In a speech he gave in the mid-'60s, Hobbs deplored various schools of advertising current at the time:

> The School for the Deaf with its credo of "Let's be so loud and annoying that people will go out and buy the product just to get out of the house and get a little peace and quiet" . . . the School of Hard Knocks, in which men in white coats hit the customer on the head with little hammers and slash through his sinuses . . . and the School for the Physically Handicapped, headed by the Man with the Eye Patch, which led to the British School, where every layout had to be exactly like every other layout, and all of them copied religiously from the Book of David.

The creative alliance between Hobbs and Goldman was not an easy one. Markedly different personalities and different approaches to advertising sometimes brought them into disagreement.

The year following Hobbs's arrival, Bill Hesse was named chief executive officer. At the annual stockholders' meeting following his election, the ex-court star came onto the stage dribbling a basketball. "I can still lay them up," he said, "but my legs give out." One of his first actions upon assuming the post was to address himself to the problem of the bilateral leadership in the creative department. It was evident by then to everybody that two head honchos was one too many. Coincidental with this problem was another one: pressure from the creative supervisors to reorganize the department vertically.

This meant dismantling the art and production departments and assigning to each supervisor his or her own complement of creative people. Many agencies had adopted this kind of vertical structure, which seemed to promise a cozier creative climate. (It also created a series of autonomous cells or agencies-within-the-agency, which presented problems.)

In mid-1965, Hesse took two actions that he hoped would solve both problems in the creative department: he assigned all copy and production people to eight vertical groups; and he set up a special creative task force called HPW which consisted of Whit Hobbs, and the two former heads of the art and production departments, Bob Pliskin and Gordon Webber, with Jack Springer as a writer. Goldman, the winner in this latest executive sparring match (his fight-manager father would have been proud of him) was made executive vice-president and remained creative director.

HPW, slightly to the left of the creative mainstream, operated as troubleshooter, firefighter and general creative handyman for about two and a half years. Its assignments were usually jobs some other creative group had struck out on—cases of chronic or terminal illness. Quite often they involved new products—it did the introductory campaigns for Vicks Nyquil and Post's Pebbles. Brainstorming with blue cards on which we wrote down every idea that came into our heads (which Hobbs pinned to his wall where they were allowed to "ripen"), we frequently did the whole job: wrote the strategy, the advertising, named the product, designed the package.*

HPW shut up shop at the end of 1967, blown away by another corporate change.

The creative reshuffling of the mid-'60s didn't take the agency's mind off the main business at hand, which was to reach the billing goal of $150 million it had set for itself in 1958. An aggressive new business push under the direction of Joe McMahon, Jr., and sparked by the salesmanship of Bill Hesse and Bob Lusk, netted sev-

---

*Bob Pliskin, a talented designer as well as an art director, designed the slant-top aerosol can for Johnson's Glade. He and Al Remson, former B&B research man, are now the principals of The First Team, a creative service similar in function to HPW. Jack Springer has a management consultant firm, First Team Ventures.

eral major new accounts. The Beech-Nut presentation brochure, "Some Notes from an Autobiography," one of the better conceived and written "leave pieces" in the agency's history, apparently did the trick. The Port Chester company assigned six of its products to B&B in 1963. Other acquisitions during the next three-year period included Heublein, Squibb, Anderson-Clayton, Utica Club beer, Shulton, Edward Dalton, and a big Detroit plum—American Motors. New assignments also came from old clients: Scope mouthwash and Bonus detergent from Procter & Gamble; Cool Whip dessert topping and Orange Plus from General Foods; and two cold-remedy products from Vicks, Formula 44 and Nyquil. The spurt of new business boosted billings in 1966 to an all-time high of $154 million.

The Revolving Door Period

But with all the new business and prosperity, something was wrong.

While the agency solicited and won an impressive number of blue-chip accounts, it had trouble hanging onto them. One account, Canada Dry, came and left within a year. Eastern Airlines flew out the window a few weeks after it had flown in. Perhaps the growth was too rapid. Perhaps the agency was too preoccupied with its internal organizational problems. It had restructured its management areas, but what was needed was something more than an orderly organizational chart. Whatever the reasons, top management began to hear complaints from clients about the service they were getting, and accounts kept slipping away.

In the five-year period 1962–67, of thirteen new accounts the agency lost eight, plus seven older ones: American Express, Philip Morris, MONY, IBM, Western Union, Florida Citrus and Instant Maxwell House Coffee. The loss of the instant coffee business hurt almost as much as the loss of Tide, for this was a product B&B had introduced and nurtured from a struggling brand to the leader in its field.

One account was resigned by Bill Hesse because of the way the client treated the agency's account people. Dick Casey recalls the circumstances of another loss, American Motors:

"AMC was having financial problems in 1967. There even were rumors that it might fold. Bill Hesse got worried about the three million bucks in media bills outstanding on the account, flew out to Detroit and asked them to go on a cash-in-advance basis. Roy Chapin (AMC president) didn't care for that. They didn't say much at the time, but about a month later they paid us a surprise visit in New York. I remember the day they arrived at 666, Chapin and Bill Luneberg, the chairman. They marched past my office with grim faces, on their way to see Hesse. They told Bill that if B&B didn't have confidence in AMC's ability to pay its bills, they'd better find another agency. They went to Wells Rich Greene."

"The TWA Touch"

In July 1967 B&B learned it was one of eight agencies invited to solicit the TWA account, then at Foote, Cone & Belding. There was only a 12½ percent chance of getting the account, as Hesse pointed out in an organization memo, but the stakes were high—a $17-million piece of business that would more than offset the billing losses of the past year.

Hesse and the rest of management decided to take the gamble, and the agency girded itself for an all-out effort. B&Bers were urged to book all their flights on TWA; a number of people flew to the Coast and back to get the feel of their prospective new client. All eight creative groups and HPW set to work looking for the Big Idea. HPW's was judged the winner: "The TWA Touch." In four weeks, six 35mm color commercials with jingle and special music tracks, and a score of magazine and newspaper ads were produced. Account management, media, research and promotion mounted a mind-boggling array of strategy plans, market analyses, program and media recommendations, merchandising ideas and collateral material, including a newly designed uniform for the stewardesses.

The presentation (cost: $150,000 out of B&B's own pocket) was so elaborate it was moved to MPO's biggest sound stage and rehearsed like a Broadway production.

On the appointed day the TWA representatives arrived, bleary-eyed from seven other presentations. They looked, they listened, they left, largely noncommittal. After two weeks on ten-terhooks, the agency got the word, and it was not good: TWA had decided to remain with Foote, Cone & Belding.

In a memo thanking everybody for "the excellence of the work," Hesse, an avid golfer who worried about his putting, said, "Don't be upset—sometimes it's the grain of the green that counts."

The TWA presentation was sad in the memory of many B&Bers for a reason beyond the failure to win the account. It was the first time it became publicly evident that Bob Lusk was gravely ill. For the first time, this consummately assured, articulate man, stumbled and faltered in his speech during the presentation. Some time later it was learned he had amyotrophic lateral sclerosis—Lou Gehrig's disease. By the end of the year, he resigned as chairman of the board, and Ted Steele was named to replace him. After a long illness, during which he lost his speech, Lusk died in January 1971 at the age of 69.

A Critical Reappraisal

The sharp drop in billings, from $154 million in 1966 to $144 in 1967 with further losses in prospect for 1968, spread gloom and concern through the upper echelons of the agency. The loss of the $11-million American Motors account, among others, coupled with the TWA disappointment, caused many a sleepless search for reasons and solutions to the agency's problems during the long winter nights.

One man especially was concerned: Jack Bowen, by now senior vice-president and management supervisor for Procter & Gamble's toilet goods brands, and a member of the board. Bowen recalls the events of that period: "I'd been worried for some time, as a lot of other people had, about the direction the agency was going, and decided somebody had to speak up."

At Bowen's suggestion, a group of directors met at the University Club to discuss their concerns. The consensus of the group was to ask Hesse to relinquish the titles of president and chief executive officer and to become chairman of the board. Hesse already had agreed that there should be a new president, but assumed he would continue as CEO for at least another year.

When Ted Steele told him of the board's decision, Hesse chose to resign, which he did formally in a letter to the board dated February 2, 1968.* It read, in part:

> This letter represents my resignation as president, chief executive officer and member of the board . . . I earnestly believe that superb officers are in place in all key capacities, and that the agency is well staffed in depth for the future. All good fortune to you.
>
> It is not my plan to re-enter the agency business in any way, shape or form. Consequently, it will be my pleasure to pull for you in any way I possibly can.

In a memo to the organization the same day, board chairman Ted Steele wrote:

> Bill's countless contributions—and the inspiration he provided us—are so well known that I should be presumptuous to comment upon them. Happily, Bill has agreed to undertake, as a consultant, several specific and important missions on behalf of Benton & Bowles.**
>
> This morning the Board of Directors elected Vic Bloede to succeed Bill Hesse as president and chief executive officer. We believe Vic to be the very personification of the qualities essential to this post. He is a young, vigorous executive who not only has served for years as our creative head, but most recently as executive vice-president and general manager for client services. . . .
>
> Under Vic's leadership we can all be confident that a most brilliant and prosperous future lies ahead for this company.

There was never much doubt that Vic Bloede would one day be president, and, eventually, chief executive officer. He had been tagged for the top job from the time he was named executive vice-president in 1964. What was not anticipated by anyone—much less Bloede himself—was that he would assume both titles at once. Tradi-

---

*On the afternoon of the same day, Marion Harper, Jr., board chairman of Interpublic, also resigned.

**After leaving B&B, Hesse was a management consultant and pursued a number of business ventures. For a number of years he has been with the American Association of Advertising Agencies, serving as interim president after the death of John Crichton in 1978. He is now executive vice-president in charge of the 4As Washington office.

tionally, the office of chief executive was reached in two stages, with a breaking-in period of a year or so as president. For the first time "the orderly progression of top management which has been characteristic of the agency," as Lusk once phrased it, was not followed.

How did Bloede feel about being struck by lightning twice at the same time?

"Scared to death," he said.

He knew the "brilliant and prosperous future" so optimistically predicted by Ted Steele was still very much in the future, and a murky one at that, and that the job of reversing the downward course of the agency wasn't going to be easy. But with the help of colleagues like Steele and Jack Bowen who soon would be named executive vice-president and manager of account services, he thought it could be done.

At a news conference held in the agency's board room, Bloede told the seventeen newspapermen present, "these are changing times in the agency business, and I think it's going to be important not only to stay abreast, but to stay ahead."

In an article covering the conference, *The New York Times* observed that while Bloede didn't expand on his statement, "he might well have meant the increasing emphasis being put these days on the so-called 'creative' ad agencies. "Mr. Hesse," the *Times* noted, "had always been on the business side. Mr. Bloede, with the agency since 1950, was formerly its top creative man."

The stressful '60s were drawing to a close. The problems the agency had lived through during the past decade still persisted—along with new ones.

But now there was new leadership. For the first time in its forty-year history the agency, still in the midst of the creative revolution, had at its helm a creative man.

Perhaps it would make a difference.

Eight

"A New Benton & Bowles"
1968–73

"*I* think the underlying lesson of these failures can be summed up in one word. That word is *complacency.*"

In his speech before the agency's annual stockholders' meeting in 1968, Vic Bloede said, "I am going to talk to you about a new Benton & Bowles," but first, he said, he was going to be "brutal about some of our mistakes of the past. In the last two years, the agency has suffered a grievous number of account losses," he said, adding that some of the losses were due to factors "beyond our control." But, he said, "the fact remains, we must have been doing *something* wrong."

To find the reasons for the loss of accounts, Bloede talked to the principals of some of the companies that had left, and got some candid opinions. They told him, he said, that, in their view, the agency had "in some cases, gotten out of touch with key client management . . . had become 9-to-5 in (its) thinking . . . had become responsive rather than innovative . . . argumentative rather than persuasive . . . selfish to suit our own needs, rather than the clients'."

What this added up to, Bloede said, was that "B&B was an agency not as hungry, not as innovative, not as aggressive, not as sensitive as it should be."

After pulling no punches on what had been wrong in the past, Bloede went on to say that B&B is still "a great agency in terms of financial strength . . . human resources . . . and clients." Although he saw formidable problems ahead, he was glad to report that present clients "are rooting hard for us." A number of them, he said, including the chairman of General Foods, the president of Anderson-Clayton and several senior people at Procter & Gamble, had expressed approval and support of the new management.

To help solve the problems of the agency and "make the most

of opportunities," Bloede announced that he and the board of directors had set up three new management committees: an executive committee consisting of Bob Lusk, Jack Bowen, Al Goldman and Dick Casey; an administrative committee made up of Frank Stanton, Bowen, Casey and Bill Holden; and a finance committee comprising Lusk, Casey, Bob Lyman and Mark Bollman.

At the same meeting Bloede announced the appointment of Jack Bowen as director of account management. "Our history has indicated," Bloede said, "that this is an area that has been a source of problems to us in the past. I have great confidence it will be in good hands under Jack's leadership."

The stockholders' meeting that year was held in the Dag Hammarskjold Theater at the United Nations Building by special arrangement as a result of the agency's Advertising Council campaign developed for UNICEF. Determined to be cheerful and optimistic, the program committee, headed by Roy Eaton, had a B&B theme song specially written for the occasion, "Moving With The Times." Copies of the lyrics were passed out to everybody and, standing in the elegant, vaulted room, the resolute voices of the 145 stockholders sang out, perhaps with more hope than conviction:

> We're gonna be moving with the times
> B&B will be moving with the times.
> We're wearing a smile on our face.
> Our batter is rounding second base.
> Our rocket is roaring into space
> Look how it climbs!
> We're moving with the times!

Brave, if somewhat corny, words. Brave expectations.

But the movement for some time was still downward. Billings in 1968 continued to drop, to $128 million, an aftermath of account losses the year before. Profit after taxes, however, *increased* 30 percent over 1967, due to staff reductions and other economies.

For the first year of Bloede's regime the job was to prevent further account erosion and begin to build a strong foundation for reversing the slide. Account service and creative were the two areas of greatest concentration.

Under Jack Bowen, account management began to strengthen relations with key client management people. Taking a page from Atherton Hobler's book, Bowen operated on the principle that if you "take care of the client's business, the client will take care of you." To help implement the program of improved client service, the board upgraded five account people to senior vice-presidents: John Anderson, Joe Hannan, Tom Hoosen, Pat McGrath and Dick Sutter. McGrath and Sutter were also elected directors.

In the creative area, Goldman named Mitch Epstein and Dick Anderson co-creative directors, and both were also elected to the board. In a move to further lift the status of creative people, an objective very much on President Bloede's mind, Gene Schinto was made copy chief, and several senior creative people were appointed associate creative directors: Joe Bacal, Ed Hannibal, Sid Lerner, Tom Ong, Liz Eddy, George Robinson, Bob Pliskin and Gordon Webber.

But with all the reshuffling and upgrading of the creative complex, after a year Bloede and the rest of management still were not satisfied everything that should be done had been done to improve the agency's creative product and its creative reputation in the industry.

A 1968 survey of how advertisers regarded a number of top agencies, including Benton & Bowles, revealed what the agency already knew: that B&B was thought to be a strong, professional marketing agency, a little conservative, and only moderately creative. Despite a spate of highly successful, highly visible campaigns—Jack Benny for Texaco's new Sky Chief gasoline;* a mass-transit poster campaign for Crest featuring celebrities such as the Mets' Ron Swoboda and the Jets' Emerson Boozer; the award-winning "Peaceable Kingdom" campaign for Chemical Bank; the mother/daughter

---

*Benny, as previously noted, was said to have been a poor ad libber, but did pretty well one time while having lunch with an associate creative director for Texaco. A devoted fan approached Benny's table, introduced herself, and said, "Mr. Benny, something's been on my mind. Why is it that all the great comedians are either Jewish or Irish?" Benny looked at her thoughtfully for a moment, then said, "Did you ever know a funny Lutheran?"

look-alike campaign for Post's Grape Nuts; and the highly publicized "Karate" commercials for Vicks Formula 44—despite advertising that was consistently doing a good job for its clients, the agency's creative image still lacked, in the eyes of the business community, the dazzle and sizzle of some of the "hot" creative agencies around town.*

So, again, the search was on. A search for a creative superstar.

There had been at least four attempts to revitalize the agency's creative department, but in none of them had there been a total commitment by top management to go all the way. None of the previous creative heads had been given the measure of authority needed to make radical changes. Through all the creative reorganizations, account management had remained firmly in the catbird seat.

But this time Bloede and his colleagues were determined to do what had never been done before. If and when the right man was found, he would be given a blank check to overhaul, rebuild and create a creative department second to none in the industry. And he would be backed by management every step of the way.

The Hampel Solution

After a wide-ranging six-month search, personally conducted by Bloede, the man finally selected was Al Hampel, senior vice-president and copy chief of Young & Rubicam, known then in advertising circles as the "hot big shop."

The first thing anyone notices about Alvin Hampel is his ready smile and quick, brown eyes—and as many a copywriter knows, those quick brown eyes can jump on a lazy dog of a sentence faster than a fox. The second thing one notices about him is his incisive wit. Little interested in small talk—he never talks about the weather—he is quick to prick the skin of pretension with a quip, a sardonic observation that gets to the truth of the matter. A third thing one notices is his clothes—his sartorial elegance is matched only by Ted Steele's—

---

*An agency's image, Al Goldman observed recently, is often based more on myth than reality. "Jean Brown (former copy supervisor) used to quote her Scottish grandfather on that subject," he said. " 'If you have a reputation for getting up at dawn, you can sleep 'til noon.' "

a taste he may have acquired from his father Leo, a former silk weaver and a pretty classy dresser himself.

One of Hampel's early advertising jobs was as promotion writer for Gulf gasoline.

"They wanted me to come up with some attention-getting signs for gas stations," he said recently. "Something that would really build traffic for the place. And that's how I came to write 'MEN.' And then I wrote 'WOMEN.' "

Hampel, whose flair for comedy writing would stand him in good stead all his advertising career, wanted to be a copywriter from the time he was a high school student in Paterson, New Jersey. Satisfying two loves—writing and clothes—he wrote a column for the school paper and worked part time in a men's clothing store. After graduating from New York University with a B.S. in marketing and a major in advertising, he got his first job with a small Paterson agency where the boss asked him only one question: "Can you use a dictionary?" He stayed there two years. When he asked for a raise, the boss refused, saying, "You'll never make it as a copywriter."

"But I got even," Hampel recalls. "I stole pencils."

He made a move toward the big time in 1954 when he got his first New York job, at Amos Parrish & Company. Three years later, after marrying Dorothy Hoanzl, he landed at Young & Rubicam, "which I looked on as Mecca," he says. While writing trade ads for Simmons mattresses, he won an award for the best trade campaign of the year, the first of a long string of awards—Clios, Gold Medals, Gold Keys and Gold Lions—won personally or for work he supervised at Y&R.

Charlie Feldman, former Y&R creative director, was his mentor. "A good man to have in your corner," Hampel says. He soon moved out of trade copy and, putting his talent for comedy to work, wrote integrated cast commercials for Jack Benny, Andy Griffith, Jim Nabors, Carol Channing and Lucille Ball. While in Hollywood on these and other assignments, he became good friends with a number of comedians, including Buddy Hackett, whom Hampel later featured in a commercial for the American Cancer Society.

In 1965, at the age of 32, he became the youngest associate

creative director in Y&R's history. Two years later he was named senior vice-president and copy chief.

Josh Levine, partner in David & Gilbert, the agency's legal firm, was the marriage broker who brought Benton & Bowles and Hampel together. To avoid any premature rumors, Hampel says, "We used to meet clandestinely at Vic's apartment where I got to know his wife Mickey and their dog Max. After a lot of conversation about my advertising philosophy and what was wrong and right about Benton & Bowles, it looked like it might be a good marriage."

Reporting the new association in *The New York Times*, Phil Dougherty wrote, "They had something in common . . . both had moved up in the business from . . . copywriting, and both were with agencies representing two of the country's biggest advertisers, Procter & Gamble and General Foods."

With the expansion of the agency's overseas operation, Al Goldman was named creative director for international. Using London, and later Brussels, as a base, for three years he worked with the creative staffs of B&B's European offices, indoctrinating them in American advertising philosophy and practices and supervising their work. He continues his long association with B&B as a client—he is now fulltime creative consultant for Vicks, doing what he likes best, working on copy strategy, among other things, with Vicks's seven agencies. A former associate says, "Al Goldman is one of the three or four best advertising strategists in the business."

Whit Hobbs returned to what he always liked best—writing. In a recent speech before the 4As, he said that too often the best writers in an agency are promoted and not allowed to write anymore. "Again and again," he said, "when a person becomes a finished writer, he or she is finished writing. That's what happened to me. They took my typewriter away . . . they sweet-talked me, they massaged my ego, they gave me my own British secretary, and my own tree . . . they made me a department head. And all I did from then on was go to meetings and whine—and play human chess—and watch all the people who were working for me have all the fun."

Currently Hobbs is back having fun as creative consultant for the *New Yorker* magazine. He lives in Greenwich, Connecticut, he says, "with one wife and two dogs in a small glass house with a helluva view—right on (and occasionally in) Long Island Sound."

The Pain of Change

About the time Al Hampel came to B&B, he read an article by a California educator in *Saturday Review* that concluded: "All change is resisted, so the question is, how can the changes be made big enough so that they have a chance to succeed."

That idea, Hampel says, became a guiding principle as he began the job of rebuilding the creative department.

The timing was right for a giant step toward a new creative *persona* for Benton & Bowles. A month before Hampel arrived, the agency made the fourth move in its history, from prestigious Fifth Avenue to workaday Third Avenue. More than a year before, it had contracted for the top eight floors of the new FDR Post Office building at 909, between 54th and 55th Streets. On June 16, 1969, under the generalship of manager of office operations Pat Duley and her assistant Vera Sands, the agency left its old files and furniture at 666 —and, it hoped, its old, conservative image—and moved into offices specially designed and decorated by Space Design, right down to the last rubber plant.* Unlike the "packing case" ambience of 666, this was an environment created especially for a modern advertising agency.

"It had become evident," said a writer in *Interior Design*, "that Benton & Bowles had shifted emphasis from more conservative advertising to highly creative work, and it was decided to inject this spirit of artistic emancipation into the physical milieu."

---

*The move was not without headaches. For the better part of a month, the newly computerized PL 8 exchange "gagged on B&B's volume of 10,000 calls a day," as *Time* put it. Incoming calls were garbled or went dead. Outgoing calls frequently ended up at a funeral parlor in the Bronx. Frustrated, the agency ran a full-page ad in *The New York Times* listing the names of all 728 B&B employees, with the headline: "These are the people you haven't been able to reach at PLaza 8-6200." The ad explained that there had been "a little phone trouble," and ended with an appeal to "keep those cards and letters coming, folks."

Recalling the ad recently, Vic Bloede said, "I had calls from the phone company and its agency before it was published asking me not to run it. But since then, they've told me the ad was a watershed in their history. It apparently shook them up enough to cause them to make major changes in the area of service and their whole approach to their business."

Put more simply, the place was a knockout: contemporary, efficient, warm and beautiful, with bold, clear colors and strong graphics accenting the black-and-white interiors.*

Exactly the right setting for a renaissance.

But before the renaissance, there was to be more than a little blood-letting.

The first problem, as Hampel saw it after moving into his handsome, contemporary corner office, was the vertical structure of the creative department that was, he said, "top-heavy with supervisory personnel." Starting at the top, the six-layer "wedding cake" looked like this: creative review board (formerly creative review committee); executive vice-president in charge of creative services; two creative directors, copy chief; associate creative directors; writers/art directors.

Hampel lopped off all the layers except ACD and copywriter/art director.

His next step was to begin reviewing all advertising so that he could get a fix on who was doing the good work. He also insisted that "no campaign is to be sent out of here without my seeing it."

The third step was more painful—restructuring the staff. During his first hundred days, Hampel replaced some 35 staffers with new people from a wide range of agencies, including several from his old shop, Y&R. "I didn't raid," he says, "they all made the first move."

If it was painful for the people who were let go, it was equally painful for Hampel. A few weeks after his arrival, he was briefly hospitalized with acute gastritis. "I was almost in a state of shock," he says, recalling the period. "This business is very quick to hire, but I don't know many people who know how to fire." He made changes, he says, only when he "was convinced that I could replace a person with a better person."

The shock was shared by a lot of people. When a popular

---

*The plan to make the top floor, with its spectacular view of the East River, the executive suite was abandoned, according to one story, when the agency's staff photographer insisted he needed an 18-foot ceiling for his studio. The executive offices ended up on the 29th floor. A year after moving in, use of the photography studio was discontinued, and the photographer was fired after running up a personal phone bill of $5,000 for long-distance calls to Alcatraz Island during the Indian occupation.

associate creative director was fired after a blowup with Hampel, a senior account man called him and said, "Hey, fella, are you sure you know what you're doing?" But nobody seriously questioned his actions, and management from the top down supported him. One writer, remembering the time, said, "You just put the blood of the lamb on your door and prayed the Angel of Death would pass you by."

But when the dust settled and the blood dried, Hampel could say, "We now stack up creatively with any shop in town, and we're equipped to handle any piece of business that comes along."

And the creative work began to bear him out. A fresh intrusiveness, a sharper competitive edge began to distinguish B&B advertising, both in TV and print. (For some time Hampel has carried on a one-man crusade for print, which he says is "underused, misused and often overlooked.")

Some highlights among campaigns produced by the "new Benton & Bowles":

Scope's "Medicine Breath" took the "Bad Breath" concept a step further by pitting the product strongly against the leader, Listerine.

Texaco's extravaganza, "Star March," with its cast of thousands was the most-talked-about commercial of 1971. The brand's filmic fable, "Tortoise and Hare" not only made a strong point about fuel conservation, it won several awards. A later Texaco commercial on the same subject featured an owl riding on a turtle.*

Pampers' print ad, headlined "The Future President of the United States Deserves a Drier Bottom," won high readership, two awards and a certificate of commendation from NOW (National Organization of Women).

Trac II's print and TV campaign made the tandem razor the biggest new product success in Gillette's history.

"When E. F. Hutton Talks, People Listen" became the most

*Producer Paul McDonough described how this improbable scene was accomplished: "Because the owl is a nocturnal bird, the trainer had to reprogram his eating habits. For two months the owl was fed only in the daytime with bits of horse meat secreted about the turtle's person, so when he was hungry, he automatically flew to the turtle. I'll bet that poor owl is still flying around Southern California looking for a turtle wearing horse meat!"

memorable slogan in brokerage-house advertising. A TV spot featuring J. Paul Getty produced by Al Hampel was memorable for a number of reasons, not the least of which was the fee paid billionaire Getty: $1.00.

The Post Grape Nuts campaign, featuring the natural food expert Euell Gibbons, gave new life to America's oldest breakfast cereal, and made a cult figure of Gibbons with the back-to-nature generation. (When the prototype Euell Gibbons commercial was presented to the Post management supervisor, his reaction was a little negative: "I don't want that dirty old man selling *my* cereal!") The campaign ran for three years until Gibbons died in 1975, and gave a healthy boost to the brand's market share.

Although Continental's cocky, colloquial headline, "We Really Move Our Tail for You," won sharp criticism from NOW, this time, for being "sexist" (you can't win 'em all), the campaign increased the flying public's awareness of the airline, and helped increase seat sales 16 percent.

"A Young, Vibrant Place"

A new spirit began to percolate through the offices and halls of 909, and B&B people were feeling it, talking about it. In a *Broadcasting* article, management supervisor and board member John Ferries said, "Benton & Bowles has changed from a rather stuffy, older and totally marketing-oriented agency to a lot more of a creative, young vibrant place."

Jerry Weinstein, who began as an art director in 1959 and is now senior vice-president and a creative group head, said, "They used to call us the dowager of the agency business, dowdy, solid but dull. We're a much younger agency now. Even the change of address made me feel differently—young and modern."

"To me an agency is like a living thing," said group executive Bern Kanner, now director in charge of international operations. " . . . Al Hampel has brought a creative dimension we didn't have before."

And news of the change began to circulate throughout the

industry. *The New York Times* advertising column reported the agency's image had changed from "a solid marketing shop that had some creative problems, to a creative shop to be reckoned with." Prospective clients began calling president Bloede. And creative people all over town began calling and writing Hampel for jobs—a sure sign of a hot shop.

With a talented, highly motivated staff turning out increasingly better advertising, and matters generally moving in the right direction, Hampel sat back one day and summed up Benton & Bowles's creative philosophy in a phrase that was to be remembered and quoted widely in advertising and business circles:

IT'S NOT CREATIVE UNLESS IT SELLS

The slogan, tailormade for a creative agency that hadn't forgotten its marketing heritage, went on buttons, brochures, T-shirts, the company's postage cancellation, matchbooks, framed samplers (hand-embroidered by Panamanian peasant women), and in full-page ads in *The New York Times*, the *Wall Street Journal* and other business publications, in which Hampel elaborated on the agency's new advertising credo.

> If anything came out of the so-called creative revolution of the 60's* and the recessions of the early 70's, it was a clearer understanding of what advertising is and what it isn't. . . . many advertisers and their agencies have been painfully reminded that advertising was not an art form but a serious business tool. And that "creative advertising" really was advertising that created sales and not just attention.
>
> During those crazy 60's . . . advertising tried to become as entertaining as the programming . . . very often at the expense of the selling idea. . . . A good joke . . . can undermine the strongest selling idea. And yet humor, judiciously used, can lift a piece of advertising . . . a good test: is the humor relevant to the message?** Advertising today

---

*Hampel once said, "Creative people used to ride in the back of the bus. Then in the '60s they rode for a while in the front. Today (the '70s) I'd say they're riding in the middle of the bus."

**As early as 1907, J. Walter Thompson, in a little booklet called "Sermons on Advertising," warned against the danger of irrelevant humor: "The mummer on New Year's Day or the clown in Barnum may look funny, but he couldn't make good on the road selling gold watches."

> must be more intrusive, more imaginative, more in-
> novative . . . In a business riddled with sameness and clut-
> ter, there is great virtue to being "creative" (but) it's not
> creative unless it sells.

The house campaign, the first in ten years, drew favorable response from advertising and business executives, even a couple of college professors. "Your ad says something that needs saying over and over again," wrote one agency chairman to Vic Bloede. A publisher of a national magazine wrote, "One of the most compelling ads I have read in years."

Even before this highly visible series of "Advertisements for Ourselves," advertisers began turning an interested eye in B&B's direction. In the first year under the new management, the agency added $16 million in new billings. First Dana, then Yardley sweetened the billings pot with several products; S. C. Johnson, Allied Chemical and Texaco, the latter under the wing of management supervisor Joe Hannan, added new assignments; and B&B got back into the coffee business with Brim decaffeinated coffee from General Foods. A concerted new business campaign netted several new accounts during the following two years: Hasbro Toys, Avis Rent A Car, Klopman Mills, Peter Paul, Kent cigarettes, Gillette's Trac II, The Kitchens of Sara Lee, and two accounts in the financial and insurance fields, E. F. Hutton and Crum and Forster, both the responsibility of management supervisor David Kreinik. In addition to his account responsibilities, Kreinik for four years was the New York coordinator of the international operation.

As the agency moved into the '70s, expansion, both domestic and international, became a key corporate objective.

Domestic Expansion

The winning of California-based Continental Airlines over thirty competing agencies opened the West for B&B. The agency had had a production office in Hollywood since *Showboat* moved to the Coast in 1937. Under Al Kaye and various other managers through the years—Bill Baker, Ted Steele, Murray Bolen, Bill Craig—it supervised coast-originated radio and TV shows. When California became an important production center for television commercials, producer Max Bryer, known affectionately as "The Silver Fox" to a generation of production people, moved from New York to Hollywood and eventually headed the office. Bryer now has his own production company, The Bryer Patch, in Hollywood.

With the acquisition of Continental, the Los Angeles office became a full service operation under Ted Burnett as general manager.* John La Pick was creative director, Ben Campisi art director, Bill Evans associate media director and Art Schulman associate research director. In 1977 Chet Lane became West Coast creative director.

In 1972, Medicus Communications was established as a subsidiary, with Ed Dent as president; Bill Castagnoli, executive vice-president and creative services director; and Larry Lesser, senior vice-president.

"Health industries look like a growing business" said Vic Bloede in announcing the newly formed subsidiary, "and their need for advertising and marketing will grow with them." A communications group specializing in the marketing of health care products to professional audiences (physicians, dentists, pharmacists, dieticians, and others), Medicus grew from $4.5-million billings in the first eight months of its operation to $27 million in 1978. Its clients include Procter & Gamble Professional Services, Vicks Toiletries Products, Schering Corporation, Morton Salt, Oral-B (Cooper Laboratories), Best Foods and Siemens Corporation. Taking a cue from its parent company, Medicus has added three subsidiaries of its own: Kissiloff Associates, a graphic arts and industrial design operation, which designed B&B Media's new home on the 23rd floor; Science and Medicine Publishing Company; and Cinemed Systems which specializes in audio-visual projects for the health care field.

Medicus, which began with nineteen people on staff, now has 77. Ed Dent retired at the end of 1978, and Larry Lesser became president and chief executive officer.

---

*Burnett, a "prodigal son" who returned, originally joined B&B in 1962, left in 1966. He was general manager of the Los Angeles office of McCann-Erickson before rejoining the agency.

Committed from an early date to the philosophy of a full-service agency, B&B took another step in 1974 to expand that capability by acquiring a majority interest in the White Plains graphics firm, Ted Colangelo Associates. TCA, headed by Ted Colangelo, whose father was a graphics man before him, designs and produces corporate and promotional literature, annual reports, identity programs, direct mail, packaging, displays and exhibits, audio-visual presentations and sales meetings.

Its roster of clients reads like *Fortune*'s 500: General Foods, Texaco, AT&T, Pepsico, Dictaphone, IBM, Xerox, Fiat, Toshiba. In 1978 TCA's net sales were $4.3 million, more than a 300 percent increase since 1974.

The agency's first Chicago office, established in 1937, had a short life—after two years the principals, Sherman and Marquette, split off and set up their own shop. Thirty-six years later the agency was back in Chicago on a firm and healthy basis. Four senior people from Needham, Harper & Steers who originally wanted to break away and form their own agency, ended up as Benton & Bowles-Chicago. Dale Landsman, Robert Cohen, John Pavasars and Thomas Papenek, all "home grown" Chicagoans, began with bright prospects but zero billing. By 1978 the agency had 45 employees and its accounts included two divisions of AMF, Johnson Products, and new product assignments from Sara Lee and Schlitz. George Simko, group executive in New York, supervises the operation, and Bill Lund, formerly of Leo Burnett, was named senior vice-president and general manager in 1979. Billings in 1978 were approximately $10 million.

Moving Into the World

"We sold our interest in our first Paris venture," Ted Steele said recently, "for $1.00—and were damned glad to get out!"

The $500-million multinational agency Benton & Bowles was to become had a late, slow beginning on the international front.

"Lusk and Hobe always dragged their feet on international expansion," recalls Steele, who moved into the international operation in 1961 and became chairman of B&B International in 1968.

"Three years after we acquired Lambe & Robinson in London, we finally had a deal to buy a minority interest in the Paris agency, Liger-Beaumont—our former associate George Beaumont was a co-partner. I was on my way over to sign the contract when Lusk called to say we'd lost the Tide account, and would have to retrench. So I had the unpleasant job of telling George the deal was off."

In 1966 affiliations were made with McKim in Toronto, and with Publicontrol in Brussels now N.V. Benton & Bowles S.A. With Andre Kicq as managing director, N.V. B&B is Belgium's second largest agency, with billings in 1978 of more than $20 million.

The ill-fated French connection, Steele explained, "was part of the Brussels arrangement. Kicq, owner of Publicontrol, also had an interest in Liger-Beaumont, and insisted we make it a package deal."

The Paris association was not a happy one. "Two years later, with $250,000 down the drain," Steele says, "we decided to cut our losses. At a very acrimonious meeting in London called to discuss a separation agreement, Beaumont facetiously offered to give us $1.00 for our interest. Back in New York, we decided to bail out, and cabled Beaumont: OFFER OF $1.00 ACCEPTED."

A highly successful Paris association was finally forged in 1977 with GRP, a holding company consisting of three agencies: Benton & Bowles Publicite/Feldman, Calleux Associates; and Concurrance (GRP/Contraste). The GRP agencies rank eighth in France, with total billings in 1978 of $47 million.

In 1972 Benton & Bowles und Partners was added to the agency's international network with offices in Frankfurt, Hamburg and Munich. Billings in 1978 were $50 million.

Today Benton & Bowles has 23 offices in fourteen countries in Europe, North and South America, with affiliates in the Middle East and Far East. The company is presently represented in areas accounting for 80-85 percent of the world's advertising expenditures.

Each of the agency's international companies operates under the same basic principles as Benton & Bowles USA: commitment to the concept of the full-service agency; total involvement in the client's business; assumption of responsibility for the productivity of the advertising it creates; and a dedication to high ethical standards in relations with clients, suppliers, the media, employees and the public. While the parent company exercises management control, the managing directors of the individual agencies are chief executive officers in every sense of the word, and run their own business.

The international network of agencies, one of the fastest growing in the world (1978 billings amounted to $258 million), serves both international and domestic clients, with national advertisers accounting for about 70 percent of the billing.

Vic Bloede is now (1979) chairman of Benton & Bowles International, and Bern Kanner director in charge of international operations. Jerry Seisfeld is inter-agency affairs executive.*

On The Move

A springtime spirit of confidence and hope animated the annual stockholders' meeting in April 1971, held again at the United Nations Building. The 135 stockholders present heard Ted Steele make an important announcement: the board had elected Vic Bloede chairman of the board, and Jack Bowen president. Bloede remained chief executive officer. Steele was named chairman of the executive committee, replacing Bob Lusk who had died the previous January.

Behind the scenes of the presentations that followed, Art Richards, Harvey Zuckerman and Irv Osowsky of the audio-visual department saw to it that comptroller Bob Lyman's financial slides and Al Hampel's reel of choice commercials were projected with nary a missed cue. Before Lyman's detailed presentation, Bloede gave the highlights of the year's fiscal news: net profits for 1970 had climbed 24 percent over 1969. And despite the recession, domestic billings were up 2.3 percent to $139 million; total billings, including international, reached $218.7 million.

During the cocktail hour, Paul McDonough, in his customary

---

*Managing directors of the major B&B international agencies: Argentina: Hernan Mayer; Belgium: Andre Kicq; Canada: Rupert Brendon; Denmark: Igor Theilade; France: Jean Feldman; Germany: Rudolf Stilcken and Dr. Hans Messing; Italy: Arcangelo Fiorani; Netherlands: Thijs Riechelmann; Norway: Magnus Eide; Spain: Juan Fontcuberta; Trinidad: Mrs. Joyce Beston; United Kingdom: Bruce Rhodes.

Ex-bombardier Vic Bloede joined B&B in 1950 as a copywriter, then rose to director of creative services before moving to account management. In 1969 he became president and chief executive officer, the agency's first president with a creative background.

Jack Bowen began his working career as a clerk in Tom Irish's grocery store in Scarsdale, New York. He was named executive vice-president and director of account management in 1968, president in 1971, and added the title of chief executive officer in 1974.

Ex-pro-basketball player Bill Hesse became president in 1962, chief executive officer three years later. He resigned in 1968, and is now executive vice-president of the American Association of Advertising Agencies, in charge of its Washington office.

Trust your car
to the man who
wears the star

TEXACO

Texaco joined the B&B family in 1961. "Trust Your Car to the Man Who Wears the Star" became the most memorable slogan in oil company advertising.

Special effect for Instant Maxwell House's "Cup-and-a-half of flavor" campaign in 1961. It took six months and $150,000 to pull it off.

General Foods' Brim decaffeinated coffee came to the agency in 1969.

Bill Tyler joined B&B as director of creative services in 1958, was named executive vice-president a year later. He resigned in 1962. A well-known critic of advertising, his column has been a long-time feature in Advertising Age.

Whit Hobbs, ex-copy chief of BBDO, came to B&B in 1963 as senior vice-president in charge of creative services. Later he headed special creative task force, HPW (Hobbs, Bob Pliskin, Gordon Webber). He resigned in 1969, is now creative consultant for the New Yorker magazine.

Al Goldman joined B&B as creative supervisor in 1959, eventually becoming director of creative services. After three years as international creative director, he left to become full-time creative consultant for Vick Chemical Company.

"Please Don't Squeeze the Charmin" is one of the most talked about campaigns in advertising history. The character of Mr. Whipple, created by the agency and played by Dick Wilson, was rated third-best-known American in a 1978 poll, after President Nixon and Billy Graham.

Another memorable TV campaign, for Vicks Formula 44 Cough Syrup, featuring Odd Job from the movie "Goldfinger," who karate-chopped to kindling everything near him when seized with a coughing fit.

Atherton and Ruth Hobler's 50th wedding anniversary was celebrated by members of the board of directors, their wives, and other friends, April 20, 1964.

Sarah Tucker, another character created by the agency, as spokeswoman for General Foods' Cool Whip.

It's not creative unless it sells.

If anything came out of the so-called creative revolution of the 60's and the recessions of the early 70's, it was a clearer understanding of what advertising is and what it isn't.

By the time those years were over, many advertisers and their agencies had been painfully reminded that advertising was not an art form but a serious business tool. And that "creative advertising" really was advertising that created sales and not just attention.

You might say creativity grew up in those years. And one would think that the mistakes made then would never again be repeated.

Yet here we are, a short time later, and like war and politics, advertising seems to be repeating itself. You need only look at television or pick up a magazine to see the frivolities and ambiguities that are passing as creative selling.

It seems such a pity that many advertisers are still learning—the hard way—what some of us have always known:

Not an entertainment medium.

During those crazy 60's, the ambience of television rubbed off on the advertising message and more and more advertising tried to become as entertaining as the programming in which it appeared—very often at the expense of the selling idea. One can still see a rash of imitative commercials following the advent of popular new television programs and feature films. Extravagant production featuring everything but a concept are still prevalent. Movie stars and athletes continue to se as substitutes for selling ideas.

Awards for what.

Awards for creativity conferred by juries of vertising people often have nothing to do with advertising that sells. Certainly, in recent years, importance of advertising awards has diminished Their value seems to have decreased in direct pro tion to the proliferation of festivals. At the same time, many began to question the worth of honor bestowed out of context of sales results.

But as long as advertising will continue to b written by people, people will continue to give e other awards. And that isn't all bad. George Bur once said of Al Jolson, "It was easy enough to make him happy. You just had to cheer him for b fast, applaud wildly for lunch, and give him a standing ovation for dinner."

You don't have to be loved.

Criticism of an advertising campaign has lit bearing on selling effectiveness. There are many examples of advertising which are disliked by the people who are reacting to the message.

By the same token, much advertising that is

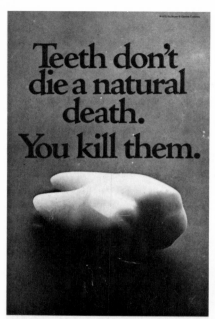

Teeth don't die a natural death. You kill them.

Chances are, when you lose a tooth, it's because you killed it with neglect. By not eating the right foods, or seeing the dentist often enough, or brushing properly.

Such neglect can lead to cavities, and cavities can lead to tooth loss. In fact, the average person loses 6 to 9 teeth in a lifetime simply due to cavities.

Crest with fluoride fights cavities. So,

besides seeing your dentist and watching treats, make sure you brush with Crest.

Because the more you fight cavities, the less your teeth have to fight for their lives.

Fighting cavities is the whole idea behind Crest.

Television is Crest's primary medium, but the brand also used print in the early '70s to reinforce its leadership position.

J. Paul Getty, one of many celebrities used by the agency in advertising for its clients.

Euell Gibbons, natural food authority, helped reenergize Post Grape Nuts.

Edward G. Robinson, an earlier celebrity spokesman for Instant Maxwell House Coffee.

Roy Bostock, group executive and director of account management, began as a trainee in 1964.

Group executive Bern Kanner, another mailroom-to-executive suite product, is director of international operation.

The agency had a little phone trouble when it moved into its new quarters at 909 Third Avenue in 1969. This ad in The New York Times shook up the phone company, sparking changes in its approach to customer service.

Group executive Bob Lyman joined B&B in 1966, became chief financial officer in 1968.

George Simko began as a media buyer in 1960, then advanced to director of media ten years later. He became a group executive in 1976.

The campaign that won the Continental Airlines account over thirty competitors. To handle business, the agency established a full-service office in Hollywood, headed by Ted Burnett.

"Ducks & Danes" for Gravy Train: first of a long series of agency-produced campaigns starring various forms of animal life.

Group executive Sandy Sulcer, "new boy on the block," came to the agency in 1977 from Needham, Harper & Steers, where he was chairman of NH&S International. He's in charge of new business and other development.

Jack Taylor, a "second-time-arounder," came to B&B in 1957, left for Ogilvy & Mather, then returned a year later. As group executive, he oversees the General Foods accounts and Medicus Communications.

A timely restaging of the Aesop's tortoise-and-hare fable for Texaco, dramatizing the do's and don't's of fuel economy.

Even a pair of eager beavers get into the act. In TV campaign for McCulloch, an account acquired in 1976, they're very much impressed with McCulloch power saws.

This ad won Pampers and B&B a letter of commendation from the National Organization for Women (NOW).

What better running mate for ex-peanut farmer Carter? Planters' Peanuts ad ran in the election year 1976.

One of the award-winning animated TV commercials for AMF's corporate advertising effort, featuring its line of leisure time products.

Demonstrations are the heart and soul of much successful television advertising. This one for Procter & Gamble's Zest helped build solid franchise for the brand.

B&B creative executives: 1979. From left: creative group heads Ed Caffrey, Frank DiGiacomo, Ron Frankel; manager of creative services Loretta Wakuya; creative group heads Donn Resnick, Richard Levenson, Joel Harrison, Jerry Weinstein; executive vice president, director of creative services worldwide Al Hampel.

Marine Midland's strong slogan has helped create awareness for the bank, is also used in bank display material.

Vicks Nyquil nighttime colds remedy was introduced by the agency in 1966, becoming the most successful colds remedy in twenty years.

The board of directors, April 1979. Seated, from left: Bob Lyman, Bern Kanner, Jack Bowen, Vic Bloede, Ted Dunn. Standing, from left: Roy Bostock, Jack Taylor, George Simko, Sandy Sulcer, Mike Moore, John Ferries, Joe Hannan, Bud Johnson. Not present: Al Hampel and Ted Burnett.

Atherton Hobler's 80th birthday luncheon in 1970. From left: Marie Scotti, Jack Bowen's former secretary; Lillian Korupp, Hobler's secretary; Helen Scofield, former secretary to Clarence Goshorn and Bob Lusk; Marion Matisse, receptionist; Hobler; Myrtle Selders, Ted Steele's former secretary; Sylvia Usher, Vic Bloede's secretary.

Three who guided the agency's destiny during early '70s: From left: Ted Steele, Jack Bowen, Vic Bloede.

role, entertained at the piano, topping off his performance as usual with "Alexander's Ragtime Band" played on his knees, wearing mittens. Altogether, it was a night for celebration, and the B&B family members, inspirited by free booze and Bloede and Lyman's good news, threw themselves into it as they sat down at tables of ten to shrimp cocktail, tournedos Henry IV, potatoes noisette, green salad, baked Alaska and two wines, with background music by the Bill Evans Trio. Although there was no reprise of the stockholders' song of '68, "We're Gonna Be Moving With the Times," the feeling in the air was that the "Gonna" was gone, and that B&B was in fact really on the move.

April that year was notable in other ways. Continuing to accent the creative, management gave eight associate creative directors the title of senior vice-president. Al Hampel, explaining the promotions with a wink said, "We had eight fewer senior VPs than the account group."

In programming, the fifteenth anniversaries of *As The World Turns* and *The Edge of Night* were celebrated at a gala reception atop the New York Hilton, hosted by CBS and Procter & Gamble. Among the 300 guests were the casts of both shows; Mary Harris, producer of *World*; *Edge* producer Nick Nicholson; Fred Bartholomew, then director of daytime programming; Ruth Levine, head of B&B casting and casting director of *Edge*; Ed Lotspiech, then P&G's general advertising manager (now retired); Mayor John Lindsay (now retired); and a longtime fan of *Edge*, the late novelist P. G. Wodehouse.

The Fight for "Freedom to Advertise"

Reporters were being jailed for refusing to reveal their news sources.

CBS "out-takes" were subpoenaed in the "Selling of the Pentagon" case.

The Nixon White House tried to restrain *The New York Times* from publishing "The Pentagon Papers."

In the climate of intimidation and threat of the early '70s, various arms of the government, in the opinion of many critics, were making grave inroads in the basic freedom guaranteed by the First Amendment—the freedom of speech and press.

Vic Bloede saw another threat from government, equally worrisome: its attack on what he called the "freedom to advertise."

In a widely reported speech before the annual convention of the American Newspaper Publishers Association in April 1973, Bloede urged the press not only to be vigilant of its own freedom, but of advertising's freedom "to carry out its function of fulfilling the public's right to know." Describing the growing trend toward regulation and control of advertising by the FTC, FCC and other regulatory bodies, he said advertisers were "threatened with being told what they can and cannot advertise . . . what they can and cannot say, and even being required to tell what their products *lack*." He cited as especially alarming the FTC's concept of "corrective advertising," and its "so-called Fairness Doctrine," which would mean that "an advertiser would become vulnerable to counter-claims prepared by Lord knows who and broadcast free of charge."

Government regulatory actions, he said, should be limited "to those dealing specifically with fraudulent material. . . . Government has no more business getting its heavy hand into such areas as humor, satire . . . and the persuasive effect of advertising copy than it does in telling a reporter how to write the lead on his story."

"It's time," Bloede declared, "to admit advertising in the First Amendment Club."

A month following the ANPA speech, Bloede was elected chairman of the American Association of Advertising Agencies, the 56th chairman since the Association's founding in 1917,* and the fight for freedom to advertise became a dominant theme of his administration. He also continued a program initiated by his predecessor, James McCaffrey, of McCaffrey & Mc Call, aimed at upgrading the public's attitude toward advertising.**

---

*Atherton Hobler, while at Gardner Advertising, was a member of the convention that founded the 4As in St. Louis in June 1917.

**The program included a speakers' bureau and a fifteen-minute film written and produced for the 4As by B&B, and filmed, in part, in its offices: "Stalking the Wild Cranberry," a documentary on the making of a Post Grape Nuts commercial, featuring Euell Gibbons.

Benton & Bowles has had a long association with the 4As, beginning with Atherton Hobler's chairmanship in 1940–41. Clarence Goshorn was chairman in 1949–50, and Bill Baker in 1954–55. Jack Bowen was a former chairman of the Association's Eastern region, and is currently (1979) director-at-large and chairman of the committee on client service.

"I guess it's time to go"

The scene was the gently vaulted, wood-paneled dining room of the University Club that stands at the corner of Fifth Avenue and 54th Street. The elegant Italian Renaissance-style building has long been a favorite gathering place for Benton & Bowles executives—Chet Bowles, Bill Benton, Atherton Hobler, Clarence Goshorn, Bill Baker, Bob Lusk, Vic Bloede, Jack Bowen have all dined and wined there with clients, other business associates and each other over many years.

Once a month during the late '60s and early '70s it was Jack Bowen's custom to have lunch with Hobler at the University Club to bring the founding chairman up to date on what was going on in the agency. Although Hobler had sold his B&B stock and no longer had an active role in the business, he still was a director and had an office at the agency. At one such lunch with Bowen in 1969, Hobler, nearing eighty, spotted at a nearby table his old former associate, the man who had taken the Colgate business from B&B nearly thirty years before and set up his own agency—Ted Bates. When Bates left, he stopped at Hobler and Bowen's table to say hello. As he walked away, Hobler leaned over and whispered to Bowen, "Don't you think he's beginning to look a little old?"

A few months later, Bowen was having another monthly lunch with Hobler at the University Club. He'd been given the unpleasant assignment of telling Hobler of a decision recently made by the board.

After a little talk about the business, Bowen finally brought up the delicate subject.

"Hobe," he said, "the directors have reluctantly come to the decision that maybe it's time you gave up your place on the board."

The old man said nothing for a moment. He'd been a director since Bowen was five years old, ever since the first board was formed when Benton & Bowles was incorporated in 1932. In the early days, board meetings were held informally in his office as the need arose, with no more notice than a holler down the hall to his colleagues. Now they were formal affairs held in a board room forty feet long, presided over by a chairman with a silver-banded gavel.

"I understand," Hobler said at last. "You need room for somebody else coming up." He looked at Bowen, his intense brown eyes now a little faded, a little less intense.

"Yes," he said, "I guess it's time to go."

On September 2, 1970, on his eightieth birthday, Atherton W. Hobler resigned from the board of directors of Benton & Bowles, and was named director emeritus. On the same day. A. M. Gilbert— "Gil" —his old friend and counselor for more than a third of a century of the advertising wars, also resigned and was made a director emeritus.

It Was a Very Good Year

"The best year in the 43-year history of our company."

The 1973 "Sharecroppers' Ball" as an early, irreverent copywriter named Lee Beulow used to call the stockholders' meetings, was held in the Time-Life auditorium, and the news from Vic Bloede was very good, indeed. B&B's total billings, domestic and international, were more than $269 million in 1972. Domestically, they had climbed to $160, up 13 percent over 1971. Net profits were up 37 percent.

Al Hampel, after a year of creative work even a tough critic like himself could be proud of, said he was determined to show every single commercial and print ad made by the agency during the year. And he did just that, with a film made by producer Ernie Motyl, a virtuoso bit of filmmaking consisting of split second scenes from hundreds of commercials and ads quick-cut to the year's big record hit, "Dueling Banjoes."

The mood of this annual meeting was markedly different from the one four years before. Anxious hope had been replaced by a sense of hard-won accomplishment. And the facts, the figures and the faces of the B&B family reflected the dramatic change.

"We have strengthened our position with our key clients," Bloede said, " . . . received new assignments from our oldest and largest clients . . . introduced major new products . . . and enjoyed important growth in new business."

In October 1973, Ted Steele sent a memo to the organization which read, in part: "After nearly 37 rewarding years with Benton & Bowles . . . I think the time has come for me to retire from our business. . . . I should like to express my heartfelt appreciation to all of the members of the B&B family—at home and abroad—for their support and for all they have contributed to my experience, both in business and in personal friendships."

Steele, who had been a key figure in management for many years, would be missed by many, including Vic Bloede. In an organization memo, Bloede wrote: "I can think of no one who has contributed more over the years to our company, its people and its welfare. . . . From a personal standpoint, I will always be grateful to Ted for his wise counsel and warm friendship during my years as chief executive."

In January 1974 Jack Bowen was elected chief executive officer. In making the announcement, Chairman Bloede said, "In his fifteen years with Benton & Bowles, Jack has made countless contributions. . . . In the judgment of our board and our shareholders, he is ideally equipped to lead Benton & Bowles to new high levels of success."

At that year's stockholders' meeting in April, Bloede was able to report another "biggest year in our history." Domestic billings were up 8 percent to $172 million, and total billings, including a 27 percent increase in international billing, were $310 million.

The "new Benton & Bowles" Vic Bloede had hypothesized six years before had taken on the solid substance of reality. Under his stewardship B&B had accomplished the almost impossible: not only reversed a disastrous decline, but risen to new levels of prosperity. Beyond that, and equally important, the team of Bloede, Bowen and Hampel had invigorated the agency with a new spirit and purpose, even given it a new character. It had come close to doing what the leopard cannot do—changed its spots. It was still a strong marketing agency—that was in its P&G genes, and always would be. But now it was something more: an agency that could stack its creative credentials up against those of any shop in town.

Now, under the leadership of Jack Bowen, a man who in all his 47 years never knew any other way but up, Benton & Bowles was set for a quantum leap in growth undreamed of by even the wildest of optimists.

Nine

"We Know Where We're Going"
1974–78

"*T*he advertising agency man," wrote Fairfax Cone in his autobiography, *With All Its Faults*, "lives much of his time on a tight wire that stretches thinly between hope and despair."

Jack Bowen has spent a good share of his time as president and chief executive officer of Benton & Bowles in trying to maximize the hope and minimize the despair. If there always will be an element of the unpredictable in the normal course of agency life, some measure of its uncertainties have been, if not eliminated, at least reduced at B&B by the prudent management and imaginative planning that has been the hallmark of his administration.

One of the points brought out in Vic Bloede's talks with the heads of lost accounts was that the agency tended to be "responsive rather than innovative." Jack Bowen was determined to correct this tendency by reordering and strengthening the management structure, and inaugurating a comprehensive program of planning for the future.

As early as 1971, as director of account management, Bowen had taken a decisive step toward better managed, more efficient client service when he conceived and put into operation the core group system, a planning body formed for each individual product or service. Comprised of top representatives of account management, creative, media and research, the core group brought key people together at the very beginning of a campaign or new account assignment, "so that no one would be working in a vacuum," as Bowen described it. The core group was first used on the Gillette account in the successful introduction of Trac II, and was steadily expanded to cover most of the agency's accounts.

Another Bowen innovation was the quarterly senior management meetings at which management people discussed various account, creative and operations problems, exchanged views and generally got things off their chest.

In another step toward better management of its own and its clients' businesses, Bowen initiated annual plans for every account in the shop which, for the first time, put down on paper how the accounts should be handled, outlined objectives and defined responsibilities. A strong believer in delegating responsibility, Bowen in 1976 named five senior management people group executives, each with his own corporate bailiwick, reporting to him. A sixth was added in 1977.

But looking ahead one year was not far enough when it came to managing the agency's own affairs, Bowen decided. In 1974, B&B adopted a six-year plan which set down in some detail the objectives for future growth and development of the company in terms of billings increases, profit and international expansion. By 1977, half-way through the plan, the agency could report a 43 percent gain in gross income, the third largest growth in revenue, after J. Walter Thompson and Young & Rubicam, in the industry, and the largest revenue percentage growth of any major agency.

A year later, the objectives of the plan not only had been met but were exceeded, and Bowen asked five of the group executives—George Simko, Roy Bostock, Bob Lyman, Sandy Sulcer and Bern Kanner—to develop a new plan. "Goals and Strategies 1979–83" defined five objectives for the next half decade: provide an unsurpassed level of quality of service to its clients; achieve an annual increase in gross income and profit of 10 percent; achieve a profit margin of 20 percent on domestic business; achieve enough profit to pay stock dividends and put aside a "nest egg"; and increase revenues from the company's international operation at an average annual increase of about 10 percent, with a profit margin of 15 percent.

A keystone of the five-year plan, and any other plan for the agency's growth and development, is the projected source and application of funds—the financial forecast, a vital aspect of agency life that has been the province of Bob Lyman, chief financial officer since 1968.

Vic Bloede recalls how Lyman was "discovered," as he termed it, "in the boiler room."

"One day Ed O'Neill (advertising financial control, division comptroller) of Procter & Gamble called on me. He said, 'You may not know it, but you have a problem in your financial area.' He went on to say our billing procedures were slow, that old charges sometimes weren't billed for eight months or a year, that generally there were a lot of billing delinquencies. Then he said, 'Having presented you with a problem, I think I may also have a solution. You have a marvelously capable guy working in accounting who, I think, could straighten out the situation.'

'Who's that?' I asked.

'Bob Lyman.' "

Actually, Lyman was already well on the way to solving the long-standing problem of delinquent billing, which was one reason he'd been brought in as vice-president and controller. But a plug from the P&G client didn't hurt the advancement of Lyman's career one bit. A short time afterwards he was made chief financial officer.

Lyman's financial fiefdom consists of four client accounting groups headed by directors Irv Birnbaum, Al Ferrarese, Roberta Wildow and Nick Conniglio; the internal account department under Jim Pinkin, senior vice-president and treasurer; and data processing, whose director is senior vice-president Ken Ross. As a group executive, Lyman also has personnel, headed by Gil Walker, under his wing, and office operations, with John McKendry as manager.

A highly esteemed, but temperamental, member of the financial department is the IBM 371-155 which is pampered in its own climate-controlled room and which, along with its predecessors, has revolutionized the accounting functions of the agency.* Bob Lyman recalls a period in the late '60s, before the prodigious "number crunching" ability of the computer had modernized the department's systems, when the agency faced a truly staggering crisis in talent payments.

---

*Computers are also revolutionizing media planning. Media management director Mike Moore says, "Minicomputers will allow our people to experiment more with alternate media plans, and do it faster. Computer technology will eventually change the number and kinds of people in media."

"The agency had gotten so far behind in its payments to members of the talent unions (SAG and AFTRA) that we were incurring stiff penalties. Soon after I came to B&B I put Earl Rowan in charge of straightening out the problem. He and his staff of six people worked like dogs for the better part of a year, and finally got the backlog cleared away. Not many people know what a Herculean job he did—saved the agency literally hundreds of thousands of dollars. I'll always have a warm spot in my heart for Earl Rowan."

After Rowan got the system working smoothly, an actress called him one day and said, "Hey, I got my check, and there's no penalty payment added to it. How come?" He told her they'd gotten things working better, that there probably wouldn't be any more penalty payments. "Who's responsible for that?" she asked. Rowan, who originally worked at the agency but had moved to Cunningham & Walsh, told her he'd been rehired to do the job. "I wish to Christ you'd never come back!" the actress said. "I was saving those penalties to put my kids through college!"

"Do it Before You Have to"

Another kind of crisis, the copy crisis, bugbear of all advertising agencies, is certainly one reason agency people spend so much time on that "tight wire . . . between hope and despair." Jack Bowen and Al Hampel decided to do something about this chronic problem when they initiated a "back-up copy" program.

"A client suffering a protracted siege of ineffectual copy," wrote Hampel in a 1977 house ad, "is a client with a roving eye . . . the day you get a campaign approved is the day to start new work on the account. . . . Do it before you have to . . . before the trouble starts." Hampel's Rx for copy crises: Have a campaign on the air or in print nationally; a campaign "in the can," tested and ready to go; and a lot of "potentially better ideas gestating at all times."

The back-up copy program is costly to the agency, in terms of the extra creative effort required, but it pays off, Bowen believes. "It costs more money when you have a copy problem and have to solve it fast."

The Name of the New Business Game

"*Winning* is the name of the new business game," declared Jack Bowen in a speech before the Advertising Club of Fairfield County in February 1977. "Getting new business, or *not* getting it, is a matter of life or death to an agency."

Bowen spoke from painful experience. He had seen the agency endure long periods of drought when very little new business came its way. He had seen it win new business, only to lose it within a year. And, happily in recent times, he had seen the agency's ability to solicit, win and hold on to accounts grow with every passing year.

During the five years 1974–78, the agency won 23 new accounts. And never before in its history had its client roster reflected such a wide diversity of products and services.

Under director of development Tom Bohan and Ron Urich, successful presentations in 1975 won the big AMF account with some eighteen leisure-time products; the Hanes Corporation for its L'Erin cosmetics line; and Standard Brands for Planters Peanuts and other peanut products.

The next two years saw diversification broaden to include a race track (Arlington/Washington); cruise ships (Holland American); a bank (Marine Midland); chain saws (McCullough); meats (Peter Eckrich & Sons, the first meat account since Goebel in 1930); cameras (Bell & Howell); and frozen foods (Van de Kamps).

The new-business pace quickened in 1978 under the generalship of Frederick D. "Sandy" Sulcer, former president of Needham, Harper & Steers, who joined the agency in December 1977 as a group executive and member of the board of directors. With Sulcer calling the signals, the agency filled three conspicuous gaps in its client list with an automobile, a beer and an insurance account. The $12-million Fiat account, the first automobile business for the agency since American Motors departed in 1967, was won in competition with Wells Rich Greene; Sullivan, Stauffer, Colwell & Bayles; and McCaffrey & McCall. Joseph Schlitz Brewing Company, won against long odds over eleven other agencies, ended a twelve-year period on the wagon (after the departure of Utica Club in 1966); and Equitable Life put the agency back in the insurance business eleven years after the association with Mutual Life was ended. The agency also acquired Quality Bakers of America Cooperative, winning handily over seven competitors. An especially happy event of 1978 was the return, after ten years, of Anderson-Clayton & Company.

While winning is the cherished goal, sometimes there are bizarre obstacles to success. Vic Bloede recalls an incident in the early '60s: "Sometime before our association with Texaco, Bob Lusk had his eye on the big Shell account which was about to leave J. Walter Thompson. There was only one hitch: we had Conoco, an account whose billings were a fraction of Shell's. In a game of musical chairs that got pretty oily, Bob resigned Conoco to be eligible for Shell. But, to Bob's chagrin, it went instead to Ogilvy & Mather. A year later we got Texaco—much to Bob's relief."

B&B had been the loser in another musical chairs maneuver in 1957 when it made one of the most elaborate new-business presentations in its history. The $24-million Buick account was looking for a new agency and B&B was very much in the running. The day before the Buick people visited the agency's office at 444 Madison, the place was cleaned and polished until it gleamed. The tops of desks and filing cabinets were cleared off, waste baskets emptied, and all employees were told to "look busy." Everybody from Bob Lusk to Ralph the shoeshine man wore buttons that read: "B&B is Right for Buick." The Buick bigwigs came, looked and listened and seemed impressed —at least with the agency's housekeeping.

A few days later Buick announced that it had selected McCann Erickson. Marion Harper, McCann president, had flown out to Detroit and landed the account all by himself without a presentation. To do it, he had resigned the much smaller Chrysler account.

At least once in recent history, the agency resigned an account before it even got it. Jack Bowen recalls the incident:

"We were making a presentation to a well-known national wine company, and were doing a darned good job of it. But as the presentation progressed, it became more and more clear to us that these were people we simply didn't want to do business with. They were rude. Arrogant. Inattentive. Downright boorish. Suddenly I decided that I wasn't going to subject our people to this kind of demeaning, degrading relationship. So, I got up and told them we were withdrawing from the solicitation. And you know something? It was a six-million-dollar piece of business! And you know something else? After the meeting, the top man told us they were going to give us the account! In a case like this, Vince Lombardi's maxim, winning isn't everything, it's the *only* thing, is wrong. When you find you have to compromise your business principles and philosophy winning *isn't* the only thing."

"Growing Our Own"

When Jack Bowen became president in 1971, he drew up a list of four major objectives he thought the agency should move toward in the conduct of its own affairs: "High profitability, high financial rewards for our people, human rewards for our people, and ensuring that Benton & Bowles is a great place to work."

It's no accident that three out of four of these goals had to do with *people*. In placing the emphasis where he did, Bowen was following a long B&B tradition, a tradition that stretches back to Chet Bowles who, as 91-year old Clarence Francis, the agency's first client, observed, "always was looking out for the welfare of his people."

This "concern for family," as one senior executive called it, runs like a silver thread (an umbilical cord?) through all the agency's history. It has no more concrete expression than in B&B's longtime policy of "growing our own"—finding quality people, training them and steadily moving them up.

"Several other agency presidents," Vic Bloede remarked, "have told me they envied our pool of managerial talent that allowed us to promote from within."

Chairman Bloede is a prime example of a "home grown" product. He began with B&B in 1950 as a copywriter. Jack Bowen is another. He joined the agency in 1959 as a staff assistant in the marketing department.

Bern Kanner is perhaps the most "home grown" of them all. He started in the mailroom, worked his way up to director of media management, is now group executive and director of the international operation.

George Simko began as a media buyer, followed Kanner's route to the top in media, and as a group executive is responsible for all activities in media, programming, research, and PR, as well as B&B-Chicago and Ted Colangelo Associates.

Group executive Roy Bostock, John Ferries and Joe Hannan, all board members, started as account management trainees. Jack Taylor, another group executive and member of the board overseeing General Foods and Medicus Communications, joined the agency in 1957 as an account executive. Board member Bud Johnson began his B&B career as a store auditor counting packaged goods on supermarket shelves. In the creative area, Jerry Weinstein, and Ron Frankel, creative group heads, started as art director and junior copywriter respectively. Mike Moore, director of media management and a board member, got his apprenticeship as an assistant media buyer.

Of the fifteen members of the board of directors as of April 1979, eleven had been with the agency fourteen years or more, most of them beginning on a low rung of the ladder. Twelve of the sixteen management supervisors are also "home grown."

The agency for many years has had a college recruitment program, with special concentration on schools of business. It also has a "deep commitment to training," as a B&B News editor wrote, "that has earned it the reputation of being one of the best training grounds for marketing and advertising people in the city."

"We try very hard to find the best when we hire people," Jack Bowen said recently, "then do our best to help them become top professionals."

Roy Bostock, director of account management, sees the agency's recruitment and training program as the keystone of its current and future strength. "We've developed in the last four years a heightened sensitivity to the need to attract, train and move up capable young people. I don't think there's another agency in town that has people of the caliber that we have, both men and women, qualified to take on increased responsibility. Especially the women—they're terrific. I sometimes tell the men, just to needle them a little, 'Hey, the girls are doing better than the boys!' "

The B&B family, as any other family, is a multigenerational organism whose members range from 18-year-old secretaries to the 59-year-old chairman of the board. It also has its retirees, some eighty of them as of the end of 1978. As the agency enters its second half century, the anniversary parties and the retirement parties in the 33rd floor rotunda around the circular stairs become more frequent. By 1978, some thirty still-employed B&Bers had reached the quarter-century mark. Fifteen of them chalked up thirty years or more, among them art studio manager Bill Tompkins who, by the end of 1979 when he plans to retire, will have logged 42 years—the longest service of any employee in the agency's history.

Not far behind him is Grace Purdon with 38 years. She used to run the stenographic pool before the age of Xerox. For the last twenty years she has been executive secretary and den mother to music director Roy Eaton and recording supervisor Tom Hendee.*

Other thirty-plus veterans: Anna Cisar, Dorothy Curtis, Glen DeBona, Bud Ehlers, Dick Ende, Frank Kenny, Sylvester Liotta, Gertrude Lubin, John Masson, Ceil Mulrooney, Bill Noble, Mary Snyder, Jim Teague, Mary Tedaldi and Harvey Zuckerman.

The B&B family, including subsidiaries, by the end of March 1979 numbered 1,242. Worldwide the figure was 2,250, a fair increase since Bill Benton, Chet Bowles and three others began the whole thing in 1929.

Growing Our Own Copywriters

The "grow our own" policy, so successful in account management and media, was extended in a limited way to the creative department in 1978 when Al Hampel set up a training program for

---

*Wisconsin-born Hendee recently celebrated his 25th anniversary with a rotunda party at which Al Hampel extolled his talents as a sound expert, observing that Hendee began as a diamond salesman. "Diamond salesman?" Hampel asked. "And he doesn't wear a yarmulke?"

copywriters under the direction of Loretta Wakuya, manager of creative services. Traditionally, very few agencies, as Bob Purcell of the 4As points out, "take the trouble to train copywriters."

"The normal practice among agencies," says Hampel, "is to raid each other's staffs. While this does wonders for the salary level of creative people, it doesn't do a thing about solving the problem of where tomorrow's creative people are coming from."

Wakuya had four copy trainees in her first "class," three of whom moved to permanent staff jobs. Wakuya herself began as a copy cub at Young & Rubicam when Hampel was copy chief. "I saw her flower into something terrific," he said, "and decided she'd be the ideal person to run our training program."

"The business has been good to me," Wakuya says, "and I want to give something back."

In addition to Loretta Wakuya, the creative executive cadre includes seven creative group heads appointed by Hampel in a restructuring of the creative department. The others: Ed Caffrey, Ron Frankel, Frank DiGiacomo, Donn Resnick, Richard Levenson, Joel Harrison, and Jerry Weinstein.

In May 1976, Hampel became director of creative services worldwide, or as someone called him, "director of all creation." In his expanded role, he travels extensively, visiting B&B's European partner agencies, working with the various creative directors. In a B&B News interview in the summer of 1977, Hampel commented on his new job, dropping, as usual, a few quips along the way:

BBN: Is there anything unique about particular agencies?

AH: Yes. In Barcelona a client driving to B&B gets his car washed free. A junior account executive does it, I believe.

BBN: What do you hope to achieve (by your trips)?

AH: Leaving Madrid on time just once. Then to upgrade the quality of the advertising. I see the finished product and comment on what I like and don't like, saying why. . . . I also visit the offices of our overseas clients . . . there is a growing trend toward U.S. clients with international business using the same multi-national agency throughout the world.

BBN: Have you enjoyed the tourist aspects of your new role?

AH: No, it's really not enjoyable. But Pepto-Bismol helps. . . .
I love the Havana cigars that are not available here because of the Cuban embargo. But it works both ways. The Cubans can't get White Owls.

The Lion in Winter

In the early '70s, Atherton Hobler, a decade older than the century, still came into his office from Woodacres, his farm outside Princeton. His prize-winning herd of Guernseys had been sold, and his health had been failing for some years—he'd had two operations on his legs for a circulatory problem—and his mind wasn't as clear as it had been. But still his wife Ruth drove him into New York a couple of times a week, usually on Tuesdays when the strategy review board met. She'd drop him at 909 Third Avenue, then do some shopping or sit in the foyer on the 29th floor and read until it was time to drive him home.

Sometimes he'd take some of the executive secretaries to lunch —Lillian Korrup, his secretary for 37 years; Bob Lusk's former secretary, Helen Scofield; Sylvia Usher, who works for Vic Bloede; and Ted Steele's secretary, Myrtle Selders. Gil Gilbert, who retired from the board with Hobler in 1970, recalls the last year or so before his final illness.

"By that time there wasn't much for him to do at the agency, nobody consulted him. He'd sit in his office, go over a little mail, read the status reports. I used to have lunch with him now and then. I'd phone to set a date, and he'd call out to his secretary, 'Miss Korrup, look at my calendar. Am I free for lunch next Wednesday?' Of course he was always free, nobody had lunch with him much anymore. We'd go to one of his favorite restaurants, Le Moal, a block and a half up Third, taking a cab—by that time his legs were so bad it was hard for him to walk. But he had this determination to keep going to the end."

Herb Hobler, his youngest son, recently talked about his

father's last days at the Princeton Medical Center. "He was in a coma much of the time. I'd sit with him, and reach out and take his hand. Even though he was unconscious, he'd clutch it and hold on, so fiercely it would hurt. He didn't want to let go."

He died January 4, 1974 at the age of 83.

The previous year, on March 18, 1973, at the age of 73, the agency's cofounder, Bill Benton, died in his sleep in his suite in the Waldorf Towers, some nine blocks from the Chanin Building where he and Chet Bowles began the agency in 1929. A man of many talents, he left advertising to become vice-president of the University of Chicago before going into government service as Assistant Secretary of State, and later, U.S. Senator from Connecticut. He also was head of Muzak Corporation, and chairman of Encyclopaedia Britannica. In a memorandum to the organization, Ted Steele wrote: "Although he had not taken part in our business since the late '30s, he never lost interest in our progress . . . and always applauded our success . . . Bill Benton was an unforgettable man. Those of us fortunate enough to have known him will never forget him."*

"We're set to grow"

"We've demonstrated in the last three or four years that we can compete, get new business and, most important, hang onto it," said Jack Bowen recently in taking a look at the future of Benton & Bowles. "We're better managed than we used to be. We plan better for the future. We've diversified, broadened our roster of accounts to include a wider range of products and services. We've expanded into other areas of communications, and we now have full service offices in Chicago and Los Angeles. Our growth has been extraordinary, both domestically and internationally, and we're set to grow a lot more."

Where will the growth come from?

---

*In 1964, on the agency's 35th anniversary, Benton had a luncheon for the members of the board of directors, at which he presented each man with a leather-bound edition of the Encyclopaedia Britannica and a set of the World's 100 Great Books.

"Increased business from existing clients. New business, we're pursuing that very aggressively with Sandy Sulcer in charge. And from acquisitions. We're looking very seriously at a number of opportunities in related communications businesses."

George Simko sees the agency today as "a much broader, all-encompassing communications business that is able to service our clients better." Pointing out that the first objective in the agency's new five-year plan had to do with client service, he said, "The quality of the relationship with the client comes first with us. Without that, you have nothing."

Bowen's optimism about future growth is based importantly on "the depth of young talent we have, both here and abroad. With our traditional policy of promoting from within, B&B is known in the industry as a good place to work. We intend to keep it that way."

A young B&B account executive, quoted in a February 1979 article in *Media Decisions*, tends to agree. Fresh out of graduate school, he said that he had received two promotions in twelve months. "B&B is known to be one of the younger agencies. People move up quickly here."

In the ornate art deco Jade Room of the Waldorf-Astoria, the agency's 326 shareholders heard Jack Bowen in April 1979 say that "1978, our 49th year, was a humdinger." As audio-visual manager Stam Nishamura and his crew projected the numbers on the big screen, Bowen revealed that worldwide billings were up $125 million to a total of $625 million. Domestic billings rose 20 percent, to $320 million.

"The growth of B&B in 1978," he said, "was not a quirk of luck. Nor will our growth in 1979, 1980 and beyond be a matter of luck. Our 2,225-member worldwide family will make everything we plan to happen, happen. Because we have a growing diversity of services, worldwide . . . because we have a growing attractiveness for our clients and our prospects . . . because we know where we are going and how we are going to get there."

Al Hampel, after observing that "this is an historic year for Benton & Bowles, it's my tenth anniversary," grew uncharacteristically serious. He said that B&B was "far better creatively" than it had been, but that "we can do better." Urging a higher critical standard and stricter quality control of the agency's creative product, he offered a new creative slogan for 1979:

OK

IS NOT

OK

The Benton & Bowles Character

After the billings have been counted, and the profits totted up, a subject frequently discussed by senior management people on the 29th floor is the B&B character.

Is there a quality that sets B&B apart from other agencies?

If it does have a special character, and almost everyone feels that it does, what exactly is that character, and is it changing?

It's almost too simplistic, too sentimental, to try to explain the character of Benton & Bowles by saying that its people constitute a "family." Many organizations, large and small, like to think of themselves as kindly corporate parents from whom all good things flow.

But the inescapable fact, made amply evident by this history, is that Benton & Bowles indeed does have a distinct *family* character, with all the attributes, and fallibilities, of a family: traditions, sentiment, loyalties, frailties. A family grounded in the Puritan ethic and old-fashioned virtues of a Benton, a Bowles, a Hobler, and carried forward by those who followed. A family that takes pride in seeing its young people grow and prosper, and looks after its older members. ("After someone stays with us a certain number of years," says Bob Lyman, "I feel we have an obligation to take care of them.")

What is the essence of the Benton & Bowles character beneath the family façade?

"I think it's made up of two things," Vic Bloede says. "An abiding concern for people, and an uncompromising commitment to integrity."

During his 29 years at B&B Bloede says, "the difficult decisions always have been resolved in favor of people. In those rare cases in which an unworthy decision has been made, there usually has been someone around to overrule that judgment in favor of the *person*."

"It's the people, the quality of the people," says Ted Steele, "that makes B&B a special place."

"They were always willing to take me back," says Shelly Platt, producer, who left the agency twice and was twice rehired.

"Four years after retiring, I still think of B&B as my company," says Marc Becker, a 30-year man and former account supervisor on Texaco.

"It was my first home," says former program head Tom McDermott.

A retired executive says, "There's something forgiving in its nature, like a demanding but loving parent. It has what a critic said John Cheever's stories have, 'a loyalty to human beings—in spite of ourselves.' "

There are minority opinions, of course. People *do* get fired, and sometimes are bitter about it. A former associate creative director, asked to leave after 25 years, felt she'd been dealt with poorly. But if she's unhappy about leaving—she's now at another agency—she also sees B&B as unique among agencies in its close, family feeling.

The family character is perhaps most strongly perceived by people on the outside.

A media man from another agency observed, "Benton & Bowles has people who were born there, cut their eyeteeth there, learned to walk there, matured and grew there. Now those same people are running the agency."

"The agency has its own standard of ethics, its own way of doing things," said a young B&B account executive. "The chain of command is very strong, yet there is communication between senior, middle and lower management. Seldom do you see newcomers at the agency. When they do appear, their presence is detected immediately. You can tell right away when somebody is brought in from outside."

An "outsider" recently brought in at a high level (it is done occasionally) sensed immediately the family feeling, the strong regard for protocol.

"The first thing I heard after I arrived," he said, "was 'Oh, we don't do things that way' and 'That's not the B&B way.' I sometimes feel like a grafted member that still may be rejected by the parent body."

There *is* a B&B way of doing things, and management felt seriously enough about it to issue, in 1978, a booklet on the subject, *Business Ethics: Everybody's Business*, a body of principles and procedures that guide the agency's business conduct. "Honesty, integrity and fairness," Jack Bowen wrote in a foreword to the booklet, "have been more than words for the people of Benton & Bowles. They have been a part of the criteria against which every decision we make is measured."

However much the intimate, informal family feeling has changed in recent years, and there's bound to be some change as the agency grows and proliferates across the American continent and the world, Bowen and Bloede believe that concern for people and a commitment to integrity, as old-fashioned as that may sound, still will remain the bedrock of the Benton & Bowles character.

Epilogue

The following is a report of a recent visit with Chester Bowles, only surviving member of the original three principals of the agency at his home at Hayden's Point, In Essex, Connecticut.

I had driven up from New York on a bright Indian Summer day at the invitation of the Bowleses. I found the little road off Route 154 and followed it through the dense pine woods to their place on the Connecticut River, a rambling white-brick house with red out-buildings, and a lawn that runs down to the river. They built it in 1939, while Bowles was still with the agency, and it has been their home ever since.

I was greeted warmly at the door by Mrs. Bowles—"Steb" as she asked me to call her—and shown into a big living room with a fireplace at one end and a comfortable, well-lived-in air about it. She explained that Chet's illness—he has Parkinson's disease—made it difficult for him to speak above a faint whisper, and that Jamie, a young aide, would sit next to him and "interpret" anything I couldn't hear.

"I'll tell Chettie you're here," Steb said, and went into the adjoining library where Bowles sat in a wheelchair. She returned to say he'd be out presently and invited me to have coffee. I followed her to the kitchen, where she poured a mug and handed me a carton of milk from the refrigerator.

Steb is a friendly, forthright woman, deeply tanned, with gray hair. We stood in the kitchen while I drank my coffee and talked.

"We've got a lot to thank Benton & Bowles for," she said. "I've said that to Chet so many times. It gave us the means that made it possible for Chet to do the things he has in public life. I never forget that."

By the time we returned to the living room, Chet was sitting in a wing chair by the fireplace, a glass of chocolate milk in his hand. Jamie sat on a hassock at his side.

Bowles flashed his characteristic sidewise smile and warmly

shook my hand. He was older looking than in his pictures—he's 77—but his face seemed more relaxed, as if the stresses of a demanding and sometimes controversial life had drained away, leaving in his alert blue eyes an irreducible residue of the humanity of the man. His once-dark hair is now thinning and gray, and he has a white mustache. He was dressed in gray flannel slacks, brown suede shoes with crepe soles, sports jacket, and button-down Oxford cloth shirt (a faded pink one), the Brooks Brothers model he's favored since his undergraduate days at Yale.

Ellie Brandell, his secretary and "vice-president in charge of everything," as Steb calls her, sat on a sofa, and I sat on a low wicker stool directly in front of Bowles, as close as possible so I could hear him.

Before beginning the interview, I gave him a jar of wild grape jelly from a batch I'd made from grapes on my place in Montauk.

"It's made with Certo," I said. "B&B's first account."

Bowles took the jar with a broad grin, held it to the light to see the color, thanked me with his eyes.

Jamie now brought out a homemade amplifying device, a length of green rubber tubing with a small funnel at one end, which he held close to Bowles's mouth when he spoke, listening at the other end. I placed the tape recorder near Bowles, but later found that only my voice and Jamie's had been picked up. The only trace of Bowles's voice was a soft sibilance, like a faraway wind in the trees.

As I bent to hear the soft whispering voice, I had the strange sense that I had come a long way, over high mountain passes, to sit at the feet of this man, as at the feet of some Tibetan priest, and that I was about to hear the secret word, the ultimate answer to a mystery.

We talked about the early radio days, about *Showboat* which he developed in 1934, about *Young Dr. Malone*, an early daytime serial he also created and wrote for a while.

"Bill took care of the business end," he said. "I wrote the ads, the commercials and produced the shows. Spent a lot of time improving, rewriting ads, trying to make them simpler, more understandable to people."

I mentioned an early research project for Certo. I knew he and

Mrs. Bowles and the Bentons used to go out and ring doorbells in the New York area, asking housewives questions about products.

He smiled, remembering. "We'd talk to as many as 300 women, it was my first experience with how the Depression affected people. I'd see the men sitting at home, no jobs, no money, utterly dejected. It made a great impression on me. Made me want to do something about it."

Did the experience have anything to do with his decision to leave advertising and begin a career in government?

He nodded. "As early as 1933, I said, 'I want to get out of this business, do something else with my life.'"

He said he used to play a lot of golf in the early days. He had been a scratch player. He pointed to a boat model on a bookcase, the *Nordleys*, his 72-foot schooner. "We used to sail a lot, the whole family. (The Bowleses have five children.) Up and down the East coast, Bermuda, the Caribbean."

I asked him what he thought of advertising now.

He said, "Better than it used to be. Better ideas. More responsible."

I ended the interview with some greetings I had carried from people I'd talked to. Clarence Francis, retired chairman of the board of General Foods and the agency's first client, had asked me to convey his best wishes. Ted Steele had said, "Tell Chet every night of my life I thank God that he hired me."

As I packed my tape recorder to leave, Bowles signaled to Jamie that he wanted to stand. Jamie helped him to his feet, and he walked slowly with me across the room to the hall. We shook hands. Before going out the door, I turned and waved. Chet, standing very straight, again flashed the marvelous smile and gave me a spunky salute.

As I drove back through the fall colors of the Connecticut countryside, I felt I had finally traced back and found the original source of the Benton & Bowles character. Before Hobe and Goshorn, before Bill Baker, Bob Lusk, Ed Murtfeldt, Ted Steele, Vic Bloede, Jack Bowen and scores of others—before them all there was Chet Bowles, the man whose vision finally carried him beyond advertising to the broader regions of the world where, as OPA Administrator, Governor of Connecticut, Under Secretary of State under two presidents, twice Ambassador to India, he had made a career of caring about people.

Here, I realized, was the wellhead of the humanist tradition that touched and shaped the lives of so many of us at Benton & Bowles.

October 1978 —GORDON WEBBER

Notes on Sources

During the research for the book, I made extensive use of Benton & Bowles's historical files, 1929–79; B&B *Bulletin,* 1947–61; B&B *News,* 1968–79; the Agency's public relations files; the B&B library's file on Agency personnel; Frank Smith's files of historical material, 1929–69; William Benton's letters to his mother, Emma Benton, 1929–35; Atherton Hobler's business files, 1932–73; miscellaneous company documents, including letters, organization memoranda, new-business brochures, promotion pieces, house advertisements and speeches; and my own files from the period 1948–75.

An essential source of information were the interviews, conversations and correspondence with the following people: Vicky Amon, Ann Bachner, Vic Bloede, Brown Bolté, Roy Bostock, Jack Bowen, Chester Bowles, Steb Bowles, Ellie Brandell, Jim Carroll, Dick Casey, John Childs, Walter Connelly, Dorothy Curtis, Steve Davis, Gail DeGroat, Ted Dunn, Rita Dunphy, Roy Eaton, Dick Ende, Rosalie Fasano, Andy Fescina, Clarence Francis, Gil Gilbert, Alice Goldberg, Al Goldman.

Also, Jim Haines, Al Hampel, Tom Hendee, Whit Hobbs, Herb Hobler, Randy Hobler, Austin Johnson, Bud Johnson, Sid Lerner, Ruth Levine, Ray Lind, Bob Lyman, George Magagnoli, John Masson, Tom McDermott, Paul McDonough, Len McKenzie, Ed Mead, Mike Moore, Ceil Mulrooney, Irv Osowsky, Pat Pattison, Dick Pinkham, Bob Pliskin, Bob Povey.

Also, Minor Raymond, Lee Rich, Art Richards, Jim Rogers, Ken Ross, Earl Rowan, Gene Schinto, Ed Schneeberg, Bill Schneider, Helen Scofield, Howard Shank, Alan Sidnam, George Simko, Frank Smith, Mert Sowerby, Dr. David Speer, Al Stanford, Al Stauderman, Ted Steele, Sandy Sulcer, Bill Tompkins, Gil Walker, Jerry Weinstein, Onnie Williams, Harvey Zuckerman.

Other sources, published and unpublished, include the following:

Chapter One

Page 11: *The New York Times,* July 15, 1929. 12: Tape of Martha

Deane radio show, May 14, 1940; 12 f: *The Lives of William Benton*, Sidney Hyman, University of Chicago Press, 1969. 13: *Me and Other Advertising Geniuses*, Charlie Brower, Doubleday, 1974. 13 f: *Lives*; 14: *Promises to Keep*, Chester Bowles, Harper & Row, 1971. 15 f: *Lives: Adventures in Advertising*, John Orr Young, Harper, 1948. 18 f: *History of Benton & Bowles*, 1929–38, Chet Dudley, unpublished. 20 f: "William Benton," Martin Mayer, *Life*, January 14, 1946; "The Four Lives of Bill Benton," Martin Mayer, *Esquire*, July, 1958. 22: Article on William Benton, Frank Gervasi, *Collier's*, June 1, 1946.

Chapter Two

Page 26 f: *The Triangle of Marketing Success*, Atherton W. Hobler, 1969, unpublished; 29: *The Lives of William Benton*. 30: *Lives*; 31 f: *Triangle*; Dudley: *History*. 32: *Promises to Keep*. 33: *Triangle*; *Lives*. 34 f: *Triangle*; *A History of Broadcasting in The United States* Vol II, *Golden Web*, Oxford University Press, 1968; *Lives*. 35 f: *Tune In Yesterday*, John Dunning, Prentice-Hall, 1976; *Lives*. 37 f: *Lives*; *Triangle*. 40 f: *Triangle*; *Lives*. 42: *Triangle*.

Chapter Three

Page 44: *Confessions of an Advertising Man*, David Ogilvy, Atheneum, 1963; Dudley: *History*. 52: *Triangle*. 53 f: *Triangle*. 55: *Dun's Review*; *Triangle*. 58 f: *Promises to Keep*.

Chapter Four

Page 60: *The New York Times*, December 11, 1950. 63: *Me and Other Advertising Geniuses*. 64: *Lives*; tape of Martha Deane radio show, May 14, 1970. 65 f: *Promises to Keep*. 76 f: *Triangle*.

Chapter Five

Page 78: *On a Note of Triumph*, Norman Corwin, Simon & Schuster,

1945. 79 f: *It Floats*, Alfred Lief, Rinehart & Company, 1958. 80: *Triangle*. 81: *It Floats; Triangle*. 82: *It Floats; Triangle; A Capsule 130-Year History of Procter & Gamble*, no date. 82 f: *Triangle*. 83: *Triangle*. 85: *The Golden Age of Television*, Max Wilk, Dell, 1976. 86 f: *Golden Age*. 88: *Business Week*, April 16, 1949. 89 f: *Golden Age*. 91 f: *How Sweet It Was*, Arthur Schulman and Roger Youman, Bonanza Books, 1976; *Only You, Dick Daring*, Merle Miller and Evan Rhodes, Sloane, 1964. 95 f: *CBS: Reflections in a Bloodshot Eye*, Robert Metz, Playboy Press, 1975; *The Golden Web*. 97: *Triangle*. 98: *Me and Other Advertising Geniuses*. 102: *Triangle; New York World-Telegram*, December 11, 1950.

Chapter Six

Page 104 f: *Broadcasting*, April 12, 1958; *New York Herald Tribune*, April 11, 1961; *Advertising Age*, April 24, 1961. 106: *Madison Avenue USA*, Martin Mayer, Harper, 1958. 109: The *New Yorker*, March 23, 1963. 113: *Triangle*. 115 f: *Advertising Age*, December 25, 1972; *More*, December 1975. 118: *Confessions of an Advertising Man*. 123: *Christianity Today*, April 1, 1971.

Chapter Seven

Page 129: *Television/Radio Age*, February 9, 1970. 131: *From Those Wonderful Folks Who Brought You Pearl Harbor*, Jerry Della Femina, Simon & Schuster, 1970; *An Analysis of Television Commercial Costs*, Manning Rubin, American Association of Advertising Agencies, 1969. 132: *Advertising Age*, July 27, 1968. 135: *The New York Times*, October 23, 1968. 136: *Broadcasting*. February 28, 1966. 142 f: *The New York Times*, February 3, 1968.

Chapter Eight

Page 148: *The New York Times*, July 20, 1970. *Time*, July 25, 1969. 149: *Interior Design*, June 1970. 150: *Advertising Age*, October 20, 1969. 151: *The New York Times*, July 12, 1970. *Madison Avenue*,

January, 1970. 152: *Broadcasting*, October 11, 1970. 153: *The New York Times*, July 12, 1970. 159: *Advertising Age*, December 7, 1964.

Chapter Nine

Page 165: *With All Its Faults*, Fairfax M. Cone, Little, Brown, 1969. *Broadcasting*, March 12, 1973. 166: *The New York Times* May 24, 1977. 171: *Broadcasting*, March 12, 1973. 173 f: *The New York Times*, April 3, 1979. 177: *Media Decisions*, February, 1979. 179: *Media Decisions*, February, 1979.

Index

N

O

With All Its Faults, 165
Wodehouse, P.G., 159
Wolf, Nort, 126
Women, employment of, 61, 133
Wonder Bread, 15
Wondra, 126n
Wood, Peggy, 89
Wylly, Dick, 83-84

X

Xerox, 156

Y

Yardley, 154
Young, Bob, 110
Young, John Orr, 15, 100

Young & Meyers, 100
Young & Rubicam, 15, 19, 39, 44, 50, 64, 100, 109, 125, 146-47, 166, 174
Young Dr. Malone, 36, 42, 182
Your True Adventure, 52
Yuban coffee, 98, 124

Z

Zander, Jack, 94
Zest, 82n, 113-14
Zest Girl, 114
Zieff, Howard, 131n
Ziff, Ruth, 112n
Zuckerman, Harvey, 158, 173

About the Author

Gordon Webber has had a 27-year apprenticeship for the job of writing a history of Benton & Bowles. He joined the agency in 1948 as its first TV copywriter, and retired in 1975 as senior vice-president and manager of the creative department. Before B&B, he was a writer and editor in the NBC television news department, and for five years a writer on the *Mama* television show. During W.W. II, he served to lieutenant (s.g.) in the Navy and received a Navy Commendation for action in the Normandy invasion. A graduate of Jamestown College (North Dakota) with an M.A. in journalism from the University of Michigan, he is the author of four novels. The latest, *The Great Buffalo Hotel*, was published by Little, Brown in May 1979. He lives in Manhattan and Montauk, Long Island.